Why It's OK
to Be a Slacker

"Stop slacking off!"

Your parents may have said this to you when you were deep into a video-gaming marathon. Or maybe your roommate said it to you when you were lounging on the couch scrolling through Instagram. You may have even said it to yourself on days you did nothing. But what is so bad about slacking? Could it be that there's nothing bad about not making yourself useful?

Against our hyper-productivity culture, Alison Suen critically interrogates our disapproval of slackers—individuals who do the bare minimum just to get by. She offers a taxonomy of slackers, analyzes common objections to slacking, and argues that each of these objections either fails or carries problematic assumptions. But while this book defends slacking, it does not promote the slacker lifestyle as the key to something better (such as cultural advancement and self-actualization), as some pro-leisure scholars have argued. In fact, Suen argues that slacking is unique precisely because it serves no noble cause. Slacking is neither a deliberate protest to social ills nor is it a path to autonomy. Slackers just slack. By examining the culture of hyper-productivity, Suen argues that it is in fact OK to be a slacker.

Alison Suen is Associate Professor of Philosophy at Iona College, New York. She is the author of *The Speaking Animal: Ethics, Language and the Human-Animal Divide* (2015) and the volume editor of *Response Ethics* (2018).

Why It's OK: The Ethics and Aesthetics of How We Live

ABOUT THE SERIES:

Philosophers often build cogent arguments for unpopular positions. Recent examples include cases against marriage and pregnancy, for treating animals as our equals, and dismissing some popular art as aesthetically inferior. What philosophers have done less often is to offer compelling arguments for widespread and established human behavior, like getting married, having children, eating animals, and going to the movies. But if one role for philosophy is to help us reflect on our lives and build sound justifications for our beliefs and actions, it seems odd that philosophers would neglect arguments for the lifestyles most people—including many philosophers—actually lead. Unfortunately, philosophers' inattention to normalcy has meant that the ways of life that define our modern societies have gone largely without defense, even as whole literatures have emerged to condemn them.

Why It's OK: The Ethics and Aesthetics of How We Live seeks to remedy that. It's a series of books that provides accessible, sound, and often new and creative arguments for widespread ethical and aesthetic values. Made up of short volumes that assume no previous knowledge of philosophy from the reader, the series recognizes that philosophy is just as important for understanding what we already believe as it is for criticizing the status quo. The series isn't meant to make us complacent about what we value; rather, it helps and challenges us to think more deeply about the values that give our daily lives meaning.

Titles in Series:

Why It's OK to Want to Be Rich

Jason Brennan

Why It's OK to Be of Two Minds

Jennifer Church

Why It's OK to Ignore Politics

Christopher Freiman

Why It's OK to Make Bad Choices

William Glod

Why It's OK to Enjoy the Work of Immoral Artists

Mary Beth Willard

Why It's OK to Speak Your Mind

Hrishikesh Joshi

Why It's OK to Be a Slacker

Alison Suen

Selected Forthcoming Titles:

Why It's OK to Get Married

Christie J. Hartley

Why It's OK to Love Bad Movies

Matthew Strohl

Why It's OK to Eat Meat

Dan C. Shahar

Why It's OK to Mind Your Own Business

Justin Tosi and Brandon Warmke

Why It's OK to Be Fat

Rekha Nath

For further information about this series, please visit: www.routledge.com/Why-Its-OK/book-series/WIOK

Why It's OK to Be a Slacker

ALISON SUEN

Why It's OK
to Be a Slacker

Routledge
Taylor & Francis Group

NEW YORK AND LONDON

First published 2021
by Routledge
52 Vanderbilt Avenue, New York, NY 10017

and by Routledge
2 Park Square, Milton Park, Abingdon, Oxon, OX14 4RN

Routledge is an imprint of the Taylor & Francis Group, an informa business

© 2021 Taylor & Francis

The right of Alison Suen to be identified as author of this work has been asserted by her in accordance with sections 77 and 78 of the Copyright, Designs and Patents Act 1988.

Library of Congress Cataloging-in-Publication Data
A catalog record for this title has been requested

ISBN: 978-0-367-72365-1 (hbk)
ISBN: 978-0-367-33818-3 (pbk)
ISBN: 978-1-003-16040-3 (ebk)

Typeset in Joanna and Din
by Deanta Global Publishing Services, Chennai, India

To Bob and Joseph—
the two hardest-working people I know

Contents

Acknowledgments

This book offers a defense of slackers. The ironic feat of laboring over the topic of slacking was made possible by my loving family. As such, I would like to thank my cat linguini, whose indifference to being useful is the source of my inspiration, Trevor M. Bibler, whose industriousness motivated me to turn an inspiration into an actual book. Without linguini, there would be no defense; without Trevor, there would be no book.

I thank my editor, Andrew Beck, for his encouragement and insightful suggestions. I thank the lively audience of my talk on slackers at Rhodes College in Fall 2019 for their excellent questions and comments. I am grateful to the anonymous referees for their helpful comments on the proposal and the manuscript. Thanks to Angela Eliopoulos for her careful reading and thoughtful editing of the manuscript.

I thank my parents, who instilled in me the importance of sleeping. As always, I thank Rebecca Tuvel for her insights, generosity, and friendship. Our conversations on slacking made this book truly a pleasure to write. A special thanks to my virtual writing group: Maya Mathur and Namrata Mitra. I will always cherish the time we spent together writing. Thanks to Garrett Z. Bredeson for his helpful suggestions on Chapter Six. Thanks to Adam Burgos for reading and commenting on Chapter Three. Thanks to the following individuals who had discussions with me at various stages of this project: Joshua

Hall, Kelly Struthers Montford, Kelly Oliver, Vanessa Tay, Chloë Taylor, and Benigno Trigo. I thank my colleagues at Iona College for their collegiality: Galen Barry, T.J. Moretti, Bonu Sengupta, Katie Smith, and Rachana Umashankar. I am grateful to be surrounded by such witty, fun, and caring colleagues. Finally, I would like to thank my wonderful friends in New York: Zareen Dadachanji, Elizabeth Edenberg, Monica Liu, and Sia Eliopoulos. Thank you for reminding me that there is still a life outside of writing this book.

In a society that promotes hyper-productivity, being a slacker makes one an outcast—or so we expect. Given our social aversion to slacking, it is nothing short of remarkable that there seem to be slackers everywhere. Many of us have encountered slackers in our lives. Perhaps it was your co-worker who seems to always be late for their shift. Perhaps it was a fellow student with whom you had the misfortune to do a group project. Perhaps it is your 30-year-old "child" who lives in your basement. Or perhaps, you are the slacker whom you have to confront every day. A cursory glance at the iPhone App Store tells us that many people are battling with their inner slackers—there is no shortage of apps that purport to curb distractions, improve time management, and ultimately increase productivity. The ubiquity of slackers, coupled with this stigma, makes slackers an interesting lot.

Indeed, my inner slacker is exactly how I got interested in this topic. Every time I put off grading papers or procrastinate over an article with a looming deadline, I ask myself, "Am I a slacker?" However, almost as soon as I posed this question, I wondered why it mattered. Who cares if I were a slacker? Who is judging me other than myself? And even if I were a slacker, why should that bother me anyway? Writing this book has given me an opportunity to think through these questions. Admittedly, there is something ironic about researching and writing a defense of slackers. When I discussed this project with my friends and colleagues, many of them commented on the incongruity of me trying to meet a deadline for a book that supposedly speaks in favor of slacking. One of my colleagues insisted that I should miss multiple deadlines if I want to be persuasive at all. (But as I will argue later, a slacker need not be a procrastinator.) Another colleague pointed out that it is not in my best interest as a professor to defend slackers, as I would be giving ammunition to my slacker students. This colleague half-jokingly prophesied that I will be getting a lot of late or subpar papers in future semesters, and I will eventually regret having written such a defense. Of course, my colleague's concern is predicated on the assumption that a *slacker* student would be motivated enough to pick up a book (not required for their course) in the first place. The scenario that my colleague envisioned—a slacker student justifying their slackness by pointing to my book, "but Professor Suen, *you* say in your book …"—is rather unlikely. I am confident that, as long as my understanding of slackers is correct, the possibility of a slacker student using my book to justify slacking is quite slim.

One particularly curious, but perhaps reassuring, sentiment I've learned while researching for this book is that I am hardly the only academic who chastises herself for being a slacker. Many of my colleagues and friends also see themselves as slackers, despite their impressive résumés. I will say more about the "self-flagellating slackers" in Chapter 2. For now, it is worth noting that slacking is interesting not just on a theoretical level, but also an existential one. For academics, the publish-or-perish model in academia means that our very professional existence depends on what we can produce. Our flexible, relatively unstructured work schedule means that we must be self-motivated and disciplined in order to get work done. The twin demands of hyper-productivity and self-discipline often give rise to unrealistic work ethic expectations. There is a constant voice in our heads reprimanding us, reminding us of the research projects that we have been neglecting, the conference proposals that we need to submit, and the pile of student papers that we should have graded last week. The taxing work of academia creates the perception that we are perpetually slacking.

I will say more about academic slackers in Chapter 4. But academic slacker is just one breed of slackers, and perhaps a rather unusual breed. For many, a slacker invokes the image of an unambitious individual whose life is devoid of aspiration. More often than not, our archetypal slacker is indifferent to their lack of a purpose in life. And this apathetic attitude is bothersome for many. After all, how could one not care about what one does or what one might become? Slackers seem particularly incorrigible because they don't even recognize their slacking as a problem. But what exactly is wrong with doing nothing or doing minimal work? How best can we understand our disapproval of slackers? Is our disapproval justified? What makes slacking different from leisure, procrastination, idleness, or laziness? These are the questions I will explore in this book.

In addition to sketching an archetypal slacker, I am also interested in the conditions under which our productivity culture can flourish. Undoubtedly, our productivity culture goes hand in hand with the rise of capitalism. Max Weber (1864–1920), a German sociologist, famously connects Protestant work ethic with capitalism.[1] He argues that the primacy of work is in part motivated by the Calvinist doctrine of predestination. The basic idea of the doctrine is the following:

whether we are saved or damned for eternity is predetermined by God, and the decision is made before we perform any deed on earth. We are "justified" before God by faith alone and not by our deeds. Interestingly, even though we don't know for certain whether God has chosen us, we still have to act *as* if we were chosen, since a "lack of self-confidence is the result of insufficient faith."[2] "Worldly activity"—work—is recommended as a way to cultivate this self-confidence and to combat religious anxiety.[3] Hard work demonstrates deep faith. So, even though hard work is not a means to salvation, it is nevertheless a "sign" of being elected by God.[4] According to Weber, this compulsive need to work (to prove our salvation), coupled with Protestant asceticism, inevitably leads to an accumulation of wealth, thereby giving rise to capitalism. Nowadays, Americans seem to have forsaken thriftiness in favor of ostentatious display of wealth, yet they continue to embrace industriousness as one of their core values.

There are many ways to analyze our productivity culture besides its economic structure and theological underpinning. For instance, we may examine the social, historical, and political conditions that enable such a culture. Given my training, I will attempt a philosophical angle in this book. I want to understand our productivity culture from an *existential* perspective. That is, I want to examine our productivity culture as we struggle to understand the (purported) nature of our being. How does work shape the way we see ourselves? Conversely, how does our conception of the self shape the way we understand work? Does being a human have anything to do with being productive? As we will see, productivity is essential not just to capitalism, but also to our subjectivity. Who we *are* and what we *do* are intertwined. The publish-or-perish model mentioned earlier vividly captures the idea that our work is constitutive of who we are—without publications, we academics can't even *be*.

We are what we do. There are many different ways for us to be productive, and there are different types of work: familial obligations, school assignments, amateur interests or projects, and so on. The job that we do to pay our rent is only one of many things that involve our labor. So, by "work" and "productivity," I am not just referring to our day job. I use the two terms more broadly to mean "doing," or things we do to make ourselves useful or accomplished (as opposed to merely to kill time). We will revisit the connection between being and doing in later chapters. For now, suffice it to say that productivity is not just about work; it is also about the kind of creature we understand ourselves to be.

A GOOD LIFE IS A LIFE OF ACTION

The primacy of doing has a long history that predates the rise of capitalism. To see how deep-seated it is, let us now turn to Aristotle (384–322 BCE), a philosopher from Ancient Greece. What would Aristotle say to someone who doesn't care to make something of themselves? As we will soon see, Aristotle believes that our very own humanity is at stake if we fail to live a life of action. In his work on ethics, *Nicomachean Ethics*, Aristotle offers a way to live a good life that puts a premium on action or activity. Aristotle is primarily interested in exploring the nature of human happiness (*eudaimonia*), the kind of good that is proper to humans. Importantly, happiness is not a mere psychological state, such as when you feel happy when you get an "A" on an exam, or when your date is going well with your love interest, or when you consume a particularly potent weed brownie. Happiness is not about being rich or living a hedonic life, nor is it about living a life honored by others. Rather, happiness is a kind of activity. Specifically, the activity of our rational soul actualizing its capacity. To understand Aristotle's idea of happiness, we need to appreciate the importance of virtue in his ethics.

To achieve happiness, we must be "virtuous." By this, Aristotle doesn't just mean being morally good. For the Greeks, "virtue" (*arete*) refers to a functional excellence; it can be applied broadly to non-moral functions or capacities. For instance, a heart surgeon is virtuous if they perform a heart surgery successfully, a violinist is virtuous if they play the violin with poise, a bartender is virtuous if they don't skimp on the alcohol. In fact, even non-humans or objects can be virtuous: a horse is virtuous if it runs fast, a chair is virtuous if it is sturdy and comfortable, even a joint can be virtuous if it gives you a smooth, relaxing high. So being virtuous means something along the lines of "performing your function well." By the same token, for humans to be virtuous, we must perform our function/capacity well. Moreover, we need to perform not just any function, but our *characteristic* function, the function that makes us who we are as humans. After all, we have a variety of functions, and not all of them are unique to us. We live and grow, but so can plants; we feel and perceive, but so can animals. A life consists merely of growing and feeling is hardly a life that we would call uniquely or properly human. For Aristotle, rationality is the function that is characteristic of humans. So, for humans to be "virtuous," we must exercise our rationality. This is why *eudaimonia* is often translated as "flourishing." Happiness—human flourishing— is achievable only when we live a life in which we actualize our rational capacity.

Action or activity plays a central role in Aristotle's conception of human flourishing. It is only by *exercising* our capacities that we may flourish, "we become just by *doing* just actions, temperate by temperate actions, and courageous by courageous actions."[5] Since human flourishing is achievable only by actions, it is not a static possession. Aristotle offers an analogy to illustrate this point, "[I]n the Olympic Games it is not the most attractive and the strongest who are crowned, but those who compete (since it is from this group that winners come), so in life it is those who act rightly who will attain what is noble and good."[6] Merely having the capacity to run fast does not get a runner an Olympic medal if they didn't participate in the game. Similarly, an individual who has the rational function but hardly employs it is not living a life proper to who they are. We cannot flourish just by having the capacity to be rational; we need to exercise such a capacity.

There is a lot to say about Aristotle's virtue ethics, but this is not a book about his ethics. For the purpose of this book, two ideas from Aristotle's ethics are of particular interest. First, a good life is a life of action. We may flourish only through *exercising* our rational faculty or *acting* rationally. Second, there is a particular way to *be* a human, a particular kind of life that is proper to who we are. Flourishing means leading a life that is worthy of who we are as humans. A good life is defined by what one does, and that we could have a good life only if we live up to what is expected of us.

For those who are familiar with Aristotle's work, it might be surprising that I am using Aristotle to illustrate the long lineage of our productivity culture. This is so because Aristotle is also known for his pro-leisure stance. He states, for example, "happiness seems to depend on leisure, because we work to have leisure, and wage war to live in peace."[7] It is clear that Aristotle considers work subordinate to leisure. As we will see, two of the pro-leisure thinkers presented in Chapter 1 trace the genealogy of leisure all the way back to Aristotle. So, perhaps it is a little misleading to present Aristotle as a forerunner of our productivity culture. Nevertheless, the tension between Aristotle's endorsement of leisure and his emphasis on actions can be resolved by clarifying what "work" means for Aristotle. As we will learn from Josef Pieper (whose defense of leisure is inspired by Aristotle), leisure is what enables us to be contemplative, to philosophize beyond the necessities of everyday life. It is precisely in our freedom from mechanical labor that we are able to flourish as humans. So, in the context of discussing leisure, the kind of work that Aristotle has in mind is primarily physical, hard labor, or labor that we perform out of necessity. While leisure is set in contrast to work, it is perfectly compatible with doing and acting. In fact, leisure is far from being idle or lackadaisical. Rather, leisure is purposeful—it is the contemplative, rational *activity* that allows us to pursue the higher, intellectual goods.

SLACKER: A DEFINITION

So what exactly is wrong with being a slacker? Why is it bad that we don't make something of ourselves? To begin answering these questions, we need to first articulate a working definition of a slacker. Here's what I propose:

1) A slacker is an individual who is underachieving; that is, they do not live up to their potential. 2) The slacker's underachievement is typically a result of their lack of, or insufficient, effort. And 3) the slacker's lack of, or insufficient, effort stems from a sense of indifference to the social expectation of making oneself useful.

Let's examine the first condition, the idea that a slacker is underachieving. It is important to note that a slacker is not necessarily someone with low achievement or lacking accomplishments. Their achievement is "low" only relative to what they could have accomplished. Put simply, they are not living up to their potential, or what is expected of them. Suppose a gifted novelist debuted their novel and it became an instant bestseller that garnered numerous accolades. This gifted novelist then decided that one successful novel is good enough, and they didn't bother to write another one. Surely, no one should deny that having a best-selling, prize-winning novel is an impressive feat, and thus the novelist is certainly not "low"-achieving by any conventional standard. But insofar as this novelist fails to accomplish more, despite having the talent, we may consider the novelist an underachiever. The other side of the same coin is that someone with low achievement is not necessarily a slacker. Suppose a student takes a calculus class but lacks the aptitude for the subject. The student may work very hard for the class and still fail it. Even though the student has low achievement in calculus, they are not a slacker.

The second condition has to do with the cause of the slacker's underachievement, which is their lack of effort. It is important to identify the cause because not all underachievers are slackers. Some underachievers may not have achieved their full potential due to circumstances beyond their control, and not for a lack of trying. Suppose a 4.0 student was on track to graduate with the highest distinction, yet unfortunately, they fell into hardship during the last semester of college. As a result, the student barely earned a passing grade in their classes during that semester. The student certainly had the aptitude to achieve a better GPA, but their underachievement is not a result of their lack of effort, and hence they are not a slacker. A slacker is someone who squanders whatever skills or talents they might have, despite having the opportunity to live up to their potential.

The third condition has to do with the *attitude* of a slacker. Specifically, their indifference to the social expectation of making oneself useful. This, I argue, is what distinguishes slacking from other forms of anti-industriousness, such as being lazy or taking shortcuts. A slacker doesn't make an effort because they are not compelled to make something of themselves. The slacker is not interested in being accomplished, having a purpose, or even just being useful. It is not that they have some principled objections against success or accomplishment— they just don't care about it one way or the other. A slacker doesn't make an effort because they don't *care*.

Before I move on, it is important to note that the slacker's apathy is specific to their personal growth and accomplishments. Although many people think of a slacker as a self-involved, lazy teenager who doesn't care about anything other than playing video games, this is a rather stereotypical caricature. Someone who cares little about their own success need not be a callous person. Undoubtedly, there are plenty of slackers who are uncaring and self-centered; but as I will argue later, such qualities are not essential to slacking. After all, plenty of slackers also love smoking pot and eating ice cream, but that doesn't mean pot or ice cream is a necessary accessory for slacking. I will address the objection regarding selfishness in more detail in Chapter 5; for now, suffice it to say that the slacker's apathy is specific to their personal achievements.

I consider this apathy to success or accomplishment to be a defining quality of a slacker. An underachieving individual who doesn't make an effort may still very much *care* about being successful and accomplished, and such an individual would not be a proper slacker. For example, a writer who doesn't publish as much as they could have because they prefer drinking all day may nevertheless feel guilty about their lack of productivity; or they may be jealous of other writers who are prolific. Despite being an underachiever due to their lack of effort, this lazy writer lacks the attitude of indifference. They care too much about success to be a slacker. Even though they may look like a slacker, they are not a slacker.

Consider another example. A student plagiarized their term paper from an academic journal, got caught, and subsequently received a failing grade. Suppose this student is bright and capable. They could have written an A paper had they made an effort. Given their aptitude, receiving a failing grade on one of their assignments is surely an underachievement. And their underachievement was a direct result of their inadequate effort, as they took a shortcut instead of putting in the hard work. Even so, taking shortcuts doesn't necessarily make one a slacker. This student who plagiarized may still on some level *care* about their academic success. Indeed, they might have plagiarized from an academic source precisely because they hope that "sounding smart" would boost their grade. A slacker student, by contrast, is indifferent to being academically accomplished. Instead of plagiarizing, a slacker student may simply turn in a low-quality paper that they scrambled to finish the night before the due date. A slacker student shoots not for a good grade, but a good enough grade to get by.

In sum, a slacker is an individual who doesn't care to make something of themselves, despite having the potential and opportunities. They don't subscribe to the idea that we should strive to be the best version of ourselves or the idea that we need a purpose or goal in life. Moreover, slacking is not just an action (or the lack thereof), but also an attitude. Without this attitude of indifference toward one's success, one is merely a slacker in appearance, but not in spirit.

SOME PRELIMINARY OBJECTIONS TO SLACKING

With this working definition, we can begin to tease out some common charges against slackers. One may find slackers objectionable because they skirt responsibilities, thereby unduly increasing the workload for others. One may also argue that even if slackers are willing to do their own share of the work, doing the bare minimum is not sufficient. Each one of us should try to contribute as much as possible to society. It is not enough to simply not impose extra work on others—we need to make positive contributions as well. By failing to pull their weight, slackers are being parasitic.

Relatedly, many believe that wasting one's talent is a disservice to others. There is a sense that a gifted individual owes it to the world to do something with their gift. A talented violinist who spends their days idling instead of practicing and performing is depriving the world of a great musician, for example. However genius they might be, someone at some point had probably taken the trouble to help the slacker cultivate their talent, be they their mentors or parents. So, by squandering their talent, the slacker is also wasting the effort of those who had invested their time and labor on them. Accordingly, a slacker is objectionable because they are selfish and ungrateful.

Setting aside the macro issue of contributing to society, some may say that it is bad to be a slacker even at a micro, personal level. For one thing, some believe that a slacker owes it to themselves to make something of themselves. The violinist who squanders their artistic talent because they couldn't bring themselves to care is doing a disservice both to the world and to themselves. For another, our sense of who we are is often informed by what we do, produce, or accomplish. We acquire our identity by actualizing our potential. If slackers are indifferent to cultivating their potential, then what they fail to produce is not simply work, but also their unique identities. As such, the problem of being a slacker goes beyond third-party harm.

I will address these concerns above in due course. For now, I will just highlight two recurring themes in this book. First, there are several philosophical attempts to defend leisure or idleness; but to a varying degree, they each have *instrumentalized* the very ideal that they seek to advocate. Second, pro-leisure thinkers have rightly criticized the way productivity culture reduces who we are to what we do; however, they continue to subscribe to the idea that there is a right way to live authentically, and we need to live accordingly in order to *be* who we are.

CHAPTER PREVIEWS

The permissibility of slacking is determined, at least in part, by *what* slacking is or who counts as a slacker. In fact, it may be difficult to make sense of some of the objections against slacking if we lack a working knowledge of a slacker. For this reason, this book is organized by two overarching questions: 1. Who is a slacker? (Chapters 2 to 4); 2. Is it OK to be one? (Chapters 5 to 7). Chapters 2 to 4 sketch a quintessential slacker, as well as their various iterations. Chapters 5 to 7 mount a defense of the slacker by entertaining different objections to slacking. Readers who are primarily interested in the defense—or readers who wish to do the minimum amount of reading—are encouraged to skip the first four chapters and the conclusion.

Chapter 1: Why Talk about Slacking?

Chapter 1 situates the topic of slacking within the larger conversation on our hyper-productivity culture. Engaging recent literature on leisure or idleness, this chapter examines six different philosophical accounts that challenge the primacy of work. Each of these accounts offers an endorsement of a form of anti-industriousness, be it leisure, loafing, idleness, or not working. For the sake of simplicity, I will call them "pro-leisure" accounts. As many of these pro-leisure thinkers point out, leisure is often co-opted to serve productivity: power naps are encouraged for the sake of working more efficiently, vacation days are instituted to avoid burnout. Under capitalism, leisure is often commodified as an instrument to optimize productivity.

To rectify such co-optations, pro-leisure thinkers argue that leisure is intrinsically valuable. Some suggest that leisure is what enables us to seek knowledge for its own sake; others emphasize the purposelessness of leisure. However, in their effort to promote leisure, many of these pro-leisure thinkers end up valorizing leisure as a preferable way of life. For some, leisure is a form of political resistance; for others, leisure is what enables us to live freely and authentically. And by assigning a higher purpose to leisure, these pro-leisure thinkers have also inadvertently instrumentalized leisure. Instead of an instrument to capitalism, leisure is now an instrument to human flourishing. As I will show, my defense of slacking differs from these pro-leisure accounts because it doesn't attempt to valorize slacking. Indeed, as long as slackers are characterized by their indifference and purposelessness, slacking resists instrumentalization.

Chapter 2: What Are the Different Types of Slackers?

Chapter 2 offers a taxonomy of slackers. It presents different types of slacking on a spectrum and argues that slacking is not an all-or-nothing affair. The three main categories I will discuss are pseudo-slackers, performative slackers, and counterculture slackers. First, a pseudo-slacker is someone who claims to be a slacker, and yet they lack the essential qualities of a slacker. The motivations of these pseudo-slackers vary. Some simply have a distorted idea of how much they work or what counts as productive or high achieving; some fake slacking as a way to show solidarity, while others fake slacking as a way to inflate their success. Second, a performative slacker is someone who flaunts their slacking. For them, slacking is a status symbol. The performative slackers use slacking as a way to show off their privileges or to gain popularity. Third, a counterculture slacker is an individual who *deliberately* chooses slacking as a way of living. For them, slacking is a critical voice against capitalism and corporate greed. The slacker counters the tyranny of productivity by refusing to be useful. Richard Linklater's 1991 film *Slacker*, for example, offers a striking depiction of this kind of a political slacker.

At first glance, the counterculture slackers may appear to be the archetypal slackers that this book seeks to articulate. After all, their slacking is neither feigned nor ostentatious. They slack because they don't buy into a productivity culture that is at the service of corporate interests. Nevertheless, I will argue that there is something ironic about being a counterculture slacker—as soon as we turn slacking into political resistance, it becomes a means to an end. However noble the end may be, slacking is once again instrumentalized.

Chapter 3: Are Hollywood Slackers Full-Fledged Slackers?

Chapter 3 turns to classical slackers we encounter in Hollywood films. Many of these Hollywood slackers are textbook slackers: they lack a life purpose, are unmotivated to change their lives, and are generally indifferent to their slacker status. I will examine three sub-categories of slackers in these Hollywood slacker films: the reformed slacker, the dissident slacker, and the slacker without a cause.

First, a popular story arc in these slacker films is the slacker's reformation. While the slacker is often depicted in an unflattering light at the beginning of the film, the plot is built around the slacker's makeover from an irresponsible lazy man-child to a productive citizen. Second, slacking is at times employed as a commentary on social ills. The dissident slackers see slacking as an alternate path to a good life, a life that is free from the tediousness and nonsense of the corporate world. Third, we have slackers without a cause. Unlike the dissident slackers, the slackers without a cause do not slack for a higher purpose. There is no heart-warming transformation story to be told, and there is no protest or resistance to capitalist ideology. If we put different types of slackers on a continuum, slackers without a cause are the full-fledged slackers that embody both the form and attitude of an authentic slacker.

Chapter 4: How Do You Spot an Academic Slacker?

Although there are slackers in every profession, Chapter 4 will focus on academic slackers, i.e., student slackers and professor slackers. Student slackers appear to be a unique breed of slackers, given that being a student is not paid work. As mentioned previously, a common charge against slackers is that slackers are not contributing to society and they are freeloaders for not pulling their weight. But in what sense is getting Cs in one's classes freeloading? And relatedly, in what sense is getting all As a meaningful "contribution" to society? This, I believe, is why we need a definition of slackers that also captures individuals who fall short of their potential, even if they are not being paid or expected to "contribute" to society.

A quintessential student slacker is best described as someone who does just enough to get a passing grade, someone who subscribes to the motto of "Cs get Degrees." Similarly, the best way to describe a professor slacker is not by citing their delinquent behaviors. Rather, much like a student slacker, a typical professor slacker is someone who does just enough to get by. Of course, unlike a student slacker, a professor does get paid for their service. So, the reasons we may find a slacker student objectionable are not necessarily the same reasons we may find a slacker professor objectionable.

Chapter 5: Is Slacking Morally Bad?

Chapter 5 addresses several charges against slacker academics that I raise in Chapter 4. These charges against slackers include: 1) slackers are parasitic and irresponsible; 2) slackers take advantage of an unfair system; and 3) slackers inflict emotional distress on others. For now, I will only say that it is important to pinpoint the qualities that we are objecting to when we criticize slackers. Are these qualities in fact essential to slacking? Or are we inadvertently objecting to qualities that are common, but merely incidental, to slacking? Recall an example I used earlier: there are plenty of slackers who like to smoke pot and eat ice cream, but that doesn't mean that pot-smoking or ice cream eating is an essential or necessary feature of slacking. Might negative qualities that we attribute to slacking be accidental, rather than intrinsic, to slacking?

Chapter 6: What If Everyone Were a Slacker?

Chapter 6 addresses the concern that slacking is not universalizable. That is, we would not want to live in a world in which everyone is a slacker. Most, if not all, of us would rather live in an enriching world than an impoverished one; and we can't have an enriching world if everyone is doing their bare minimum. Hence, slacking is objectionable because, if universalized, it would create a world that no one would rationally want to live in. This chapter will also look at a different version of the freeloading problem: the idea that the slacker is objectionable on the grounds that they fail to make a positive contribution to the world. It is not enough that the slacker doesn't impose an undue burden on others—they also have to make a positive contribution to the richness of the world.

To articulate the "what if everyone were a slacker" problem, as well as the freeloading problem, Chapter 6 will rely heavily on Enlightenment philosopher Immanuel Kant (1724–1804) as its resource. Engaging with Kant also allows us to expand a discussion in Chapter 1 on the relationship between being and doing. As I will show, there have been various philosophical attempts to promote leisure as the more authentic or dignified way of living. But the idea that anti-industriousness offers a form of existential freedom is very much indebted to the Enlightenment ideal that links productivity to subjectivity. As we will see in Chapter 6, Kant's argument explicitly links being and doing, who we are and what we do. Engaging with his argument will give us a better understanding as to why subjectivity is at the very core of our debate in productivity.

Chapter 7: Do Slackers Have an Identity Crisis?

Chapter 7 attends to the concern that a slacker's lack of life purpose may give rise to an identity crisis. Consider, for example, a typical social interaction in which two people are introduced for the first time. One of the first exchanges invariably concerns what they respectively do for a living. Given that we typically gain a sense of self through our work and accomplishments, slackers are at risk of having an existential crisis if they cannot acquire a unique identity through work. This concern focuses on first-party harm. That is, even if slackers do not wrong others, they are still doing a disservice to themselves by depriving themselves of individuality.

To address this concern, I suggest that we expand alternate ways to *be*. In addition to the things that we do, we also forge our identity through our family history, political stances, and our relationships. There are different ways by which we constitute ourselves. So, even if the slacker does not define themselves by what they do (or not do), they may still be able to acquire a solid sense of who they are through other ways. So, one way to resolve the slacker's existential crisis is by disentangling being from doing. This chapter will end with an analysis of the ways pro-leisure thinkers have appropriated the Enlightenment ideal that links productivity to subjectivity.

Conclusion: The Pandemic Slacker

As part of this book was written during the 2020 COVID-19 pandemic, the concluding chapter is a reflection of what it means to be a slacker in the age of the pandemic. Specifically, I examine our productivity culture through the lens of the pandemic. How might the new work-from-home culture affect our understanding of work and leisure, for example? What are we expected to *do* or accomplish when we are stuck at home? And given the escalating unemployment rate, how might the pandemic change public perceptions of those who don't have a job? Furthermore, this chapter will examine the role of the slacker in our "battles" against the Spanish Flu and the novel coronavirus, drawing on narratives from both the 1918 and the 2020 pandemics. By analyzing the ever-evolving pandemic narratives, I argue that slacking has, in a surprising twist, become a token of patriotism.

With the increasing awareness of our hyper-productive culture, a new genre of books promoting leisure has recently emerged. While many of them critique the normative expectations of labor and endorse varying degrees of leisure or slow living, most of these books continue to treat leisure as purposeful. For some, leisure is good because it increases productivity and creativity.[8] For others, leisure is a form of liberation, a vehicle to freedom. In short, leisure is to be endorsed because it makes our lives better.[9]

Even though I agree with many of these critiques of the American work ethic, especially its capitalist underpinnings, I believe that slacking presents a unique case for anti-industriousness. In their attempt to valorize anti-industriousness, pro-leisure thinkers inadvertently instrumentalize it. Whereas many scholars are eager to turn "not working" and "idleness" into a protest against the regime of productivity,[10] I argue that slacking is resistant to such instrumentalization. Slackers lack a purpose in life because they do not feel compelled to make something of themselves. Similarly, my account of slacking does not serve a noble purpose because slacking need not have a point. In other words, slacking need not be purposeful for it to be defensible.

This is not to deny that the life of a slacker can be desirable in its own right. Many of us find slacking attractive—not necessarily because we detest working, but rather because we crave the slacker's independence and their nonconformist spirit. The fact that a slacker does not bow to the social expectation to be useful means that they are at least free from the bondage of hyper-productivity. The slacker seems defiant and unconcerned with the judgment of others. As we will see in Chapter 7, the slacker challenges (albeit unintentionally) not just our work ethic, but also the notion that our identity is based on what we do. In fact, even the manner with which a slacker rejects the cult of productivity is unapologetic: instead of finding clever ways to defend their slackerdom, the slacker simply shrugs their shoulders. The slacker does not even feel the need to give an account for their lack of productivity. Understandably, many of us aspire to live a life where we can be freed from peer pressure. Many of us would like to think that we don't care about what other people say. Many of us would like to live defiantly and unapologetically. So, at least looking from the outside, there is something liberating—even courageous—about the slacker.

Nevertheless, I want to tread carefully here. Although there is certainly something attractive about being a slacker, I take the positive qualities of slacking to be the side effects, rather than the purposes, of slacking. As I will argue, slacking ceases to be slacking when we try to turn it into something purposeful. While I don't deny the liberatory potential of slacking, I am wary of the temptation to turn slacking into an antidote to our cultural malaise. In fact, I wonder whether slacking can still make good on its promise to "free" us from the tyranny of labor when it turns into a path to a purportedly more enlightened, authentic way of living. Can slacking still liberate when it becomes the lifestyle for which we strive?

What I offer in this book is quite modest. In keeping with the title, the main goal of this book is to examine the permissibility of being a slacker. It does not advocate slacking as an emancipatory way of living. To say, "It's OK to be a slacker" means it is *morally acceptable* to be a slacker, and not necessarily that it is advisable to be one. Granted, we do sometimes use the phrase "It's OK..." in a colloquial way to sanction an action or a situation beyond moral permissibility. Suppose

I say, "It's OK to eat two donuts!" while passing around a box of Krispy Kreme, I am likely trying to *persuade* others to take more donuts, and not merely defending the moral permissibility to having two donuts. But we also use "It's OK…" to sanction an action without encouraging it. Suppose I am at a friend's house and I want to smoke a cigarette; I may ask my friend, "Is it OK to smoke on your balcony?" And suppose my friend isn't a big fan of tobacco, they may nevertheless reply, "Yes. It's OK to smoke." In this case, my friend may sanction my smoking, even if they don't find it advisable. In this book, I am using "It's OK…" in the latter sense. Given that many people *do* judge slacking as morally problematic, it makes sense to prioritize a defense of its moral permissibility. And given the pervasiveness of our productivity culture, even a modest, limited defense of slacking is already quite an undertaking for a short book such as this one. Admittedly, my defense of slacking may be unsatisfying for some. If a reader picked up this book expecting some sort of endorsement for slacking, they would be disappointed. But as I hope to show, a modest defense (as opposed to an endorsement) is the best way to preserve the uniqueness of slacking. As such, the goal of this book is not to promote slacking as a preferable or beneficial way of living, but to show that, contrary to popular belief, it is not wrong to be a slacker. In short, it is OK—but really *just OK*—to be a slacker.

What makes slacking different from procrastinating, idling, or being lazy? Of course, a slacker may act in any or all of these ways. Yet a slacker needn't procrastinate or be idle, nor is a slacker necessarily lazy. As we have seen in the Introduction, a unique feature of slacking is the sense that slackers could have achieved more or done better, yet they don't bother to realize their potential. It is perfectly conceivable that slackers do their jobs and act responsibly, given their assigned duties, yet slackers are unmotivated to go beyond the bare minimum, even though they certainly could achieve more. In other words, slacking has to do with failing to accomplish one's potential, rather than failing to do one's duties.

Slackers don't particularly care about being a disappointment. It is typically those around them who are frustrated or infuriated by their slacking. Apathy or indifference is at the heart of slacking. This feature explains why it is difficult to be evangelical about slacking—apathy is not an attitude that one could develop simply with enough persuasion. And few slackers become slackers because they read a convincing argument about its virtues. As I will show in this chapter, it is difficult to make a pitch for slacking in the way philosophers have done with leisure.

While a slacker often conjures the image of an unemployed couch potato, it is important that we don't conflate slacking with not working. After all, not working is often the *means* to increase productivity. Mandatory time off, sabbaticals, and "nap pods" (capsules installed in an office for employees to take power naps midday) are all meant to prevent burnout, boost morale, and ultimately optimize productivity. Whereas Aristotle said in 350 BCE that we "work in order to have leisure,"[1] we now have leisure in order to work.

In a *New York Times* opinion piece titled "The 'Busy' Trap," we see clearly that leisure is at the service of work. In it, Tim Kreider makes a case against busyness. Importantly, his objection to busyness is not a critique of productivity. Rather, he is objecting to the kind of superficial busyness that we put on to make ourselves feel important—the kind of busyness that is not, in fact, conducive to our productivity. When Kreider himself fell into the busy trap, he resolved to break free by fleeing town to an "Undisclosed Location" where he was "unmolested by obligations."[2] And by getting rid of tiresome busywork such as answering emails, he was "finally getting some real writing done for the first time in months."[3] For Kreider, then, busyness is objectionable not because the demand for productivity is objectionable; quite the contrary, busyness is objectionable because it gets in the way of productivity. He writes,

> Idleness is not just a vacation, an indulgence or a vice; it is as indispensable to the brain as vitamin D is to the body, and deprived of it we suffer a mental affliction as disfiguring as rickets. The space and quiet that idleness provides is a necessary condition for standing back from life and seeing it whole, for making unexpected connections and waiting for the wild summer lightning strikes of inspiration—it is, paradoxically, necessary to getting any work done.[4]

By "idleness," Kreider does not mean being idle unproductively, given that it is in fact the means to "getting any work done." The ultimate goal of idleness is productivity. Within the capitalist regime, leisure (or idleness) is not done for its own sake—we recharge ourselves so we can work even harder, and better.[5] While the ways leisure is appropriated to service productivity and capitalism are well-documented, what we will see in this chapter is that leisure can be instrumentalized for other ends as well.

Echoing Kreider, in a more recent *New York Times* article titled "You Are Doing Something Important When You Aren't Doing Anything," Bonnie Tsui argues for the importance of "fallow time." Just as a farmer must let the land fallow to maintain its fertility, we must rest in order to work. At first glance, Tsui's thesis is reminiscent of Kreider's defense of idleness. Yet, she insists that this goes beyond boosting productivity:

> I don't mean for fallow time to be seen as just another life hack, the way that even meditation has been hijacked as something that will boost your productivity. The upside of this kind of downtime is more holistic than that—it's working toward a larger ecology of workers who are recognized as human beings instead of automatons.[6]

Notice, even here Tsui does not challenge the primacy of productivity (she seems to take our status as workers for granted). For her, it is the "ecology" of working that needs changing. Specifically, she implores us to work in a manner that reflects our humanity (as opposed to working like a machine). Even though Tsui insists that rest is not just a means to work, she continues to instrumentalize rest. Only now instead of productivity, we have "humanity" as our end goal. As we will soon see, for many thinkers, leisure is intertwined with who we are as humans. Leisure is not just about free time, it is more importantly about freedom—the kind that makes us who we are as humans. In what follows, I will offer six distinctive accounts of anti-industriousness. By engaging with recent literature on leisure and idleness, I will situate the topic of slacking within the larger conversation on our culture of hyper-productivity.

BERTRAND RUSSELL

In 1932, Bertrand Russell, one of the most well-known public intellectuals in Britain, published a short essay titled "In Praise of Idleness." A prolific scholar, Nobel Laureate, and anti-war activist, Russell was hardly the poster boy for idleness. His publications range from philosophical treaties on logic and mathematics, to an anti-nuclear manifesto (the so-called "Russell–Einstein Manifesto," as Albert Einstein was one of the signatories), to this essay on the merits of idleness. However, the essay title, like Kreider's endorsement of idleness, is regrettably misleading. What Russell advocates is not idleness in the sense of "doing nothing," but rather the *democratization* of leisure.[7] Russell also advocates for diversity in leisurely activities, specifically the need for us to take up more *active* pastimes. He believes that the exhaustion produced by long working hours explains why people often opt for "passive" pleasures such as watching movies or listening to the radio.[8] While Russell admits that everyone should work to earn their keep, he stipulates that no one should have to work for more than four hours per day.[9] The truncated workday would give us not just more time, but also more energy as we would be less likely to feel burnt out. So instead of limiting ourselves to passive entertainment, we would be more inclined to include active and strenuous pastimes.[10]

Although Russell uses "laziness," "idleness," and "leisure" interchangeably throughout the essay, what he has in mind is closer to how we ordinarily understand "leisure," the sort of activities that we do beyond our everyday necessities. Leisure affords us the opportunity to engage in an activity for its own sake, rather than for wages or survival, or as a means to some other practical ends.[11] Russell believes that the leisure class (primarily the wealthy, landowning upper class) has been indispensable to civilization. The leisure class "cultivated the arts and discovered the sciences; it wrote the books, invented the philosophies, and refined social relations."[12] Insofar as the leisure class need not concern itself with practical everyday necessities, it can rise above the "barbarism" of mundane concerns.[13]

Yet, Russell is well aware that leisure has historically been the privilege of the wealthy: the "idleness [of the leisure class] is only rendered possible by the industry of others; indeed their desire for comfortable idleness is historically the source of the whole gospel of work."[14] By singing praises to idleness, then, Russell is trying to equalize the burden of work and the privilege for leisure between the rich and the poor. For Russell, the elite class should be more industrious, not less.

While Russell's advocacy for idleness is in part a concern for fairness, it is also about the advancement of civilization. The social arrangement of having a small, elite leisure class that contributes to civilization while the rest of the population toils away is both unjust and inefficient. As he cheekily points out, the leisure class might have produced "one Darwin," but the group "as a whole was not exceptionally intelligent."[15] Why, then, should we rely on a small portion of the population for the important task of advancing culture and civilization?[16] By democratizing "idleness" and expanding the leisure class, we would be able to recruit new talent to contribute to cultural progress.

Finally, consistent with his pacifism, Russell argues that an anti-war stance is a logical extension of a leisurely life. One obvious reason is that war takes *a lot of work*—it is fundamentally at odds with a life of leisure. Another reason, according to Russell, is that a life of leisure transforms how we relate to others. A life with less work-related stress and exhaustion is a happier life. And those who live happier lives "will become more kindly and less persecuting and less inclined to view others with suspicion. The taste for war will die out."[17] As such, leisure is indispensable to both civilization and peacemaking.

JOSEF PIEPER

Fifteen years after Russell's "In Praise of Idleness," German philosopher Josef Pieper published two essays that would later become *Leisure: The Basis of Culture*. As the title of his book suggests, Pieper argues that "culture depends for its very existence on leisure."[18] Tracing the origin of the word "leisure," Pieper reminds us that the English word "school" is derived from the Greek word for leisure (σχολή)—it is from leisure that the institution for learning sprung.[19] For Pieper, the etymology of leisure is important for understanding a liberal arts education. When we pursue knowledge in leisure, we are free from the everyday concern for survival. It is this freedom from the practical or the useful that gives liberal arts its *liberty*. This liberty is even more evident when we contrast the liberal arts with "servile arts." According to Pieper, servile arts have "a purpose" that "consists in a useful effect that can be realized through the *praxis*."[20] Whereas liberal arts do not require external justification (they are valuable in and of themselves), servile arts can only be legitimated by the social function that they serve. In leisure, we are able to pursue knowledge for its own sake. We may, for example, investigate the nature of slacking not because it serves some practical purpose for us in our everyday living, but simply because it satisfies our own curiosity. Of course, this is not to say that intellectual endeavors cannot be "useful" in the ordinary sense. One may, for example, write a term paper on slacking for a philosophy class to fulfill a course requirement. But the practicality or usefulness of our pursuit of knowledge will always remain in the peripheral in the liberal arts.

Pieper further argues that the practical benefits of leisure (if there are any) are merely incidental. In a forwarding-looking passage, Pieper critiques the instrumentalization of leisure prevalent in today's productivity discourse:

> leisure is not there for the sake of work, no matter how much new strength the one who resumes working may gain from it; leisure in our sense is not justified by providing bodily renewal or even mental refreshment to lend new vigor to further work—although it does indeed bring such things![21]

As mentioned above, within the neoliberal capitalist regime, leisure has been co-opted to enhance productivity and corporate performance. But as Pieper argues here, while leisure may increase productivity, that is merely a side effect, rather than the purpose, of having leisure. Just as the pursuit of knowledge (in the liberal arts) need not be justified by its pragmatic function, our need for leisure is not grounded in whether it helps us work more.

Like Russell, Pieper believes that we need leisure to rise above the mundane. Though unlike Russell, Pieper takes great pains to detach leisure from idleness. Idleness should not be conflated with leisure because it is in fact *antithetical* to leisure. Tracing the meaning of idleness back to the High Middle Ages, Pieper insists that "the restlessness of work-for-work's-sake arose from nothing other than idleness."[22] While the connection between idleness and restlessness may seem counter-intuitive at first glance, consider how the rise of smartphones has changed our idle moments. We check our text messages while waiting in line at a coffee shop, scroll through our social media feeds during our morning and evening commutes, or swipe on dating apps in between meetings. With our smartphones, there seems to be never a dull moment. Yet, as we know, compulsive phone scrolling is hardly a fulfilling pastime. Mounting research suggests that our addiction to social media (and the internet more generally) has contributed to anxiety, depression, and low self-esteem.[23] Whereas leisure is supposed to liberate us from the tyranny of work, our idle phone scrolling is far from emancipatory. It is telling that one of the most popular website-blocking applications on the market is called "Freedom."[24] The name speaks to the sense of helplessness and the lack of self-control that many experience while browsing aimlessly on the internet. Our constant need to be connected leaves us feeling restless and unfree.

There was, of course, no internet or smartphone addiction when Pieper talked about idleness in the summer of 1947. So, the restless idleness to which Pieper objects has to do with the kind of thoughtless, empty way we live our lives. We fill our daily lives with meaningless busywork that doesn't do justice to who we really are. Although Pieper explicitly rejects the idea of using leisure as a means to provide a refreshed workforce, his objection to "restless idleness" is reminiscent of Kreider's idea that superficial busywork is getting in our way of achieving something greater.[25] As we saw above, for Kreider, meaningless busywork (such as clearing one's inbox) prevents him from being productive and doing the "real writing." For Pieper, restless idleness prevents us from becoming who we are. Even though leisure is not meant to increase productivity, it is still purposeful; and while leisure is not meant to serve capitalism, it is meant to promote human flourishing.

For Pieper, the freedom afforded by leisure is more than just free time, and the liberty that defines the liberal arts is more than just academic liberty. As we have seen, Pieper argues that leisure is what enables us to pursue knowledge beyond the necessities of everyday life. This existential freedom from the mundane is precisely what enables us to flourish as humans. Pieper calls leisure "a condition of the soul,"[26] and that leisure is possible only when we are "in harmony with" who we are.[27] In contradistinction to leisure, idleness means that

> the human being had given up on the very responsibility that comes with his dignity: that he does not want to be what God wants him to be, and that means that he does not want to be what he really, and in the ultimate sense, is.[28]

The problem of idleness, then, is not about wasting time. Rather, the problem is that we are being trapped in the realm of restless "total-work," unable to become who we are supposed to be. To reframe Pieper's words in a more secular way: when we are idle—and restless—we fail to live up to what it means to be a human with dignity.

When human dignity is at stake, we begin to see that there is something tricky about the notion of pursuing knowledge "for its own sake." We may read a book not because it serves a practical benefit such as fulfilling a course requirement or preparing for an exam. We may read a book simply because the experience of reading itself is delightful. But what happens when being at leisure becomes the mark of humanity? What happens when existential freedom becomes a *prerequisite* of being a proper human? Despite Aristotle's (and Pieper's) claim that leisure is pursued for its own sake, it is ultimately an instrument to a specific notion of human flourishing.

NICOLE SHIPPEN

While Pieper's effort to promote leisure is very much informed by Aristotle, and he repeatedly makes reference to the Greeks in his account of leisure, he doesn't go into details to investigate the social-economic underpinning that makes room for leisure in the first place. This is an unfortunate omission. As we saw above, even Russell readily acknowledges the privileged position of the leisure class. In fact, Russell's effort to promote idleness is precisely motivated by his desire to democratize leisure (or what he calls idleness). This brings us to Nicole Shippen's *Decolonizing Time: Work, Leisure, and Freedom*, a work on the politics of time where leisure takes center stage. Like Pieper, Shippen takes up Aristotle's insight that leisure is a precondition for freedom. Unlike Pieper, however, Shippen attends to the social-political conditions out of which a leisure class is rendered possible. By doing so, Shippen demonstrates the political relevance of leisure. For the purpose of this chapter, Shippen's classical understanding of leisure shows two points: 1) leisure is instrumental to who we are as humans; 2) the fight for leisure is a political issue.

For Shippen, the project of reclaiming leisure is political through and through. In addition to making concrete, on the ground changes in public policies such as universal basic income, guaranteed living wages, and reduced work hours (without reduced pay), reclaiming leisure is also important for challenging the capitalist framework on a conceptual level. It is "an important part of developing a collective critical awareness about time as *already* a political issue, and seeks to resist, confront, challenge, and ultimately transform the colonization of time by capital."[29]

Shippen seeks to reclaim a classical understanding of leisure by engaging primarily with Aristotle. For Aristotle, it all begins with the struggle between necessity and freedom. Our effort to cover basic needs constantly compromises our pursuit of freedom. For when we are bogged down by the banality of meeting our basic necessities, we do not have time, nor the energy, to engage in civic life. The answer to our negotiation between necessity and freedom, according to Aristotle, is that we should delegate work only to certain groups of people; specifically, women and slaves. A gendered and classed division of labor will then afford male citizens time for civic engagement. As such, with the "appropriate" kind of social arrangement, a selected group of individuals is able to fully immerse in the public sphere, unencumbered by the demand of mundane necessities such as cooking, cleaning, caretaking, or keeping the household in order generally.

Unsurprisingly, Shippen rejects the unjust division of labor that Aristotle endorses. Yet, she believes that Aristotle's account is especially helpful for articulating the politics of leisure. For one thing, Aristotle's account explicitly acknowledges that leisure is made possible by a specific social-economic arrangement via the political exclusion of women and slaves. For another, Aristotle's account of leisure works in tandem with a "teleological understanding of time in relationship to the development of human potential and actualization."[30] In other words, leisure is indispensable to our achieving our potential as humans.

Contra the classical account, our colloquial and "uncritical" account of leisure fails to appreciate its social-economic underpinning, as it sees leisure as a matter of mere "individual choice."[31] Under capitalism, leisure is often commodified as goods or services that an individual consumes, be it a new gaming system or a weekly cleaning service.[32] Freedom in this context is reduced to a freedom to shop. More problematically, our contemporary understanding of leisure fails to appreciate its relevance to human flourishing by conflating leisure with free time. Shippen argues that leisure is distinct from free time. First, free time is not necessarily leisurely under the capitalist regime. As we saw earlier, the kind of "rest" promoted by corporate culture is typically at the service of productivity. We rest in order to optimize productivity. Relatedly, in our overworked culture, one typically spends one's free time on recuperating from one's labor.[33] We are too burnt out to engage in taxing, yet enriching, pastimes. We are more likely to binge watch Netflix or scroll through our phone in bed during the weekends instead of training for a marathon or learning a new, challenging skill. As we saw earlier, this is why Russell advocates for shorter working hours: when we feel less burnt out from our job, we are more likely to choose the more active pastimes, thereby diversifying our leisurely activities.

Second, Shippen argues that free time spent without any purpose is just idleness, which is incompatible with the classical notion of leisure as *purposeful*, an "ideal form of temporal autonomy, or the ability to control one's time in a meaningful and self-directed way."[34] Once again we see a connection between leisure and autonomy. For both Pieper and Shippen, leisure is not just a matter of free time, but also a matter of how we are constituted as individuals.

To reclaim leisure, Shippen draws a distinction between "discretionary time" and "free time": the former refers to an individual's ability to control time in a way that allows them to develop and exercise autonomy, whereas the latter is very much constrained by the structure of capitalism.[35] Discretionary time has agency built into it, whereas free time gives us the illusion of choice. With discretionary time we enjoy leisure, with free time pseudo-leisure.

Discretionary time is typically associated with existential freedom, i.e., autonomy. Autonomy is the ability to self-govern, to live one's life according to values and purposes that one could claim as one's own. Being autonomous does not mean doing whatever you want. A smoker who is addicted to nicotine may be "free" to smoke to the extent that no one interferes with them, but they are not autonomous as long as their addiction dictates their actions. For our purpose here, we may understand autonomy as a robust freedom exercised in a thoughtful, deliberate way, as opposed to a pseudo freedom that revolves around satisfying hedonistic pleasures. Autonomy requires the ability to reflect on our choices and a conscious effort to live one's life according to one's well-considered values, whereas pseudo freedom is a mindless pursuit of gratifications of one's desires.

With discretionary time, individuals are able to engage in leisure activities that promote critical reflections, meaningful choices, and civic duties for the common good—much like male citizens in ancient Athens were able to participate in civic life in their leisure.[36] By contrast, free time is more often associated with a reductive, consumeristic pseudo freedom that flourishes under capitalism. Given our hyper-productive, overworked culture, it is hardly surprising that most people nowadays find "free time" rather than "discretionary time" outside of work. They are more likely to engage in "leisure" activities in the form of consumption (shopping, eating out, getting a massage, etc.), as opposed to leisure activities that are conducive to personal growth, critical reflection, and civic engagement.

LIN YUTANG

In 1937, Lin YuTang, a Chinese scholar who taught at Harvard University, published *The Importance of Living*. An important part of living, as it turns out, is our ability to appreciate "loafing." Like Russell and Pieper, Lin sees a link between leisure and culture: "Culture, as I understand it, is essentially a product of leisure. The art of culture is therefore essentially the art of loafing."[37] Interestingly, Lin insists that idleness "was decidedly not for the wealthy class," and that the cult of idleness was "the cult for the poor and unsuccessful and humble scholar who either had chosen the idle life or had idleness enforced upon him."[38] This is a rather peculiar point, especially when we juxtapose it with Russell's commentary of the aristocratic leisure class, and thus it deserves some consideration here.

Across dynasties, China relied on civil examinations to fill various positions in the government. Success in the exam was a major path to wealth, fame, and political power for centuries. Generations of Chinese literati submitted themselves to memorizing Confucian classics in the hope of securing a position in the government. As only a few succeeded in each exam (the national exam was held only once every three years), many scholars who tried their luck, and failed, in the exam ended up taking teaching posts elsewhere. According to

Lin, the life of idleness and leisure resonates particularly well with those who had failed to establish themselves through the path of civil examinations, "as I imagine the poor schoolmaster teaching the poor scholars these poems and essays glorifying the simple and idle life, I cannot help thinking that they must have derived an immense personal satisfaction and spiritual consolation from them."[39] Unable to obtain a position in the government, these underachieving academics coped with their disappointment by subscribing to the cult of idleness.[40] The kind of idleness that Lin has in mind is not the kind of restless idleness that Pieper detests, nor is it the kind of leisure that Russell tries to democratize, and it is certainly not a strategic withdrawal from busywork that Kreider uses to enhance productivity. Rather, idleness requires a "*detachment* toward the drama of life," it is a "high-mindedness" that allows us to develop a different kind of relationship to fame, wealth, and social status.[41] A quintessential "high-minded" individual eschews worldly success and enjoys a simple life with few material comforts.

While the underachieving scholars had idleness thrust upon them when they failed to acquire a position through civil examinations, it would be a mistake to think that idlers were just losers with a sour grapes attitude. Indeed, some of the iconic "high-minded" idlers in the history of Chinese literature voluntarily gave up their offices because they were tired of the endless responsibilities and "eternal kowtowing" that came with their supposedly prestigious position.[42] One example of such official-turned-idler is poet Tao Yuanming[43] (陶淵明, 365–427 CE), who resigned after 80 some days in the office to return to his home in the countryside. One of Tao's most celebrated works is exactly about his return home ("Homecoming"), in which he speaks of the joy of drinking alone, strolling in the garden, chitchatting with his family, and observing the four seasons. While Tao may remind us of the aristocratic leisure class that Russell finds contemptible, he was far from rich or privileged.[44] In the preface to "Homecoming," Tao speaks candidly of his motivation to seek an official position in the first place: he was poor, and his income from farming was not sufficient to provide for his large family ("the house was kid-filled, while the rice jar was empty").[45] Yet, despite this practical necessity for a well-paying job, Tao could not stay for a job that he deemed compromising: "while starving in the cold is agonizing, going against my character is what sickens me."[46]

The iconic scholar-idlers that Tao represents offer some interesting insights regarding the purpose of leisure/idling. As we have seen, Lin agrees with Russell and Pieper that culture "is a product of leisure." However, it is not immediately clear what "culture" means in this context. After all, even though many of these idlers happened to be literati, their idleness was not meant to contribute to civilization, intellectual progress, or the liberal arts (à la Russell, Pieper). Rather, as Lin points out, idleness involves developing a disposition that is "bent on seeking a perfectly useless afternoon spent in a perfectly useless manner."[47] As such, idleness seems to serve no higher purpose than allowing the literati to live a life untroubled by official responsibilities. That they happened to have produced an extensive body of literature detailing their carefree, moon-gazing life is largely incidental. The high-minded idler is admired not for making use of his talents and actualizing his potential, but for resisting the seduction of worldly success.

The high-minded idler that Lin describes is not the rich aristocrat who lives above the plebeian concern for everyday survival, nor is he a custodian of civilization or the liberal arts. Yet, there is something familiar about the narrative Lin presents here. Specifically, the idea that the high-minded idler is a *principled* idler: he is unwilling to compromise his character for a well-paying, prestigious job. We have seen a similar trope in Tsui's, Pieper's, and Shippen's accounts of leisure. For Tsui, rest is critical for work insofar as it allows us to *work with dignity*. For Pieper, leisure frees us from the trap of restless total-work, so we can live a dignified life that is proper to who we are as humans. For Shippen, it is by engaging in appropriate leisure activities that we may flourish as autonomous individuals. In Chinese literature, the high-minded idler is trading material success for his dignity—for Tao, the poet-idler, having a job that would compromise his character is worse than starving in the cold. Indeed, his reason for resigning his office was very much about defending his integrity. According to an anecdote, when asked to make a courtesy call on a visiting official (who was known for his corruption and bribery), Tao refused, "how can I bow to a yokel for the sake of five bushels of grain?"[48] The "five bushels of grain" refers to the salary and benefits Tao received as a government official. Tao was pointing out the high moral cost of keeping his job—he resigned that very same day. Since then, the idiom "not bowing for five bushels of grain" (不為五斗米折腰) has entered into Chinese vocabulary, describing honorable individuals who refuse to prostrate themselves for money. Tao's idle lifestyle has come to symbolize the dignity and freedom that are proper for an intellectual. As Lin puts it, "somehow the high-minded scholar who valued his character more than his achievements, his soul more than fame or wealth, became by common consent the highest ideal of Chinese literature."[49]

BRIAN O'CONNER

The existential freedom that anti-industriousness purportedly offers is taken up once again in Brian O'Conner's excellent and provocative book, *Idleness: A Philosophical Essay*. Engaging with Kant and his successors, O'Conner offers a compelling account of philosophers' stubborn resistance to, and skepticism of, idleness since the Enlightenment. By presenting such an account, one of his goals is to "prevent the philosophical case against idleness from having the last word."[50] While O'Conner does not present himself as an advocate of idleness,[51] he seeks to portray idleness as a reasonable way of living (or, minimally, not an irrational way of living).

Like Pieper, O'Conner is keenly aware of the ways leisure has been appropriated to service productivity. Though unlike Pieper, O'Conner insists that idleness is resistant to such appropriation (rather than complicit to it). This, of course, shows that the two have radically different understandings of idleness. Whereas for Pieper idleness is an all-consuming restlessness, for O'Conner, it is first and foremost "a feeling of noncompulsion and drift."[52] Far from restlessness, idleness is a lack of "inner power struggle in which something in us needs to be overcome or improved."[53] Idlers are those who are unmotivated to "elevate themselves into a higher level of existence."[54]

When idleness is understood in terms of a lack of purposefulness, we can begin to understand the anxiety surrounding it. The question, "What is the purpose of my life?" is asked so often that it has become a cliché. Meanwhile, seeking and answering one's calling is now a standard expectation, rather than a privilege. The presumption is that the value of one's life depends on its purpose, and a life without purpose is not a life worth living. Idleness gives us an uneasy feeling not simply because we can't get our work done. Rather, idleness troubles us because it interferes with the narrative of a meaningful life that we have long inherited and propagated.

In addition to our conception of a good, meaningful life, our subjectivity—our very conception of the self—is also on the line here. A particularly helpful feature of O'Conner's analysis of idleness is the ways he explicitly connects what we *do* to who we *are*. According to him, insofar as idleness challenges conventional notions of a good life, "the very idea of being a 'self' of the appropriate kind is thereby placed in question."[55] Our work matters to us because it helps define us. What we do matters to us because our very own identity depends on it. And if we don't do anything, our sense of self is at risk.

At the heart of the doing/being codependence is the following: as humans, we are obligated to actualize our potential so we can become who we are meant to be. Depending on the philosopher, we may get a different picture of who we are meant to be (though, becoming a rational being is a common aspiration). Nevertheless, the underlying message is the same: humanity (or what it means to be a proper human) is an achievement, rather than a given. O'Conner articulates what he calls the "worthiness myth," the "uplifting story about how we human beings can overcome those human tendencies we take to be based in nature: the greater the effort, the more impressive and worthy the result."[56] The appeal to "effort" here is significant: the process of actualization involves work—we don't just become who we are meant to be by doing nothing. Indeed, even reaching the goal in and of itself may be insufficient if we did not obtain it with effort (say, we somehow reached our goal by sheer luck or deception). After all, if we have not worked for it, we are not *worthy* of the prize. To illustrate this point, consider writing: you may have the potential to be a successful, prolific writer, but you can't be a writer unless you write. Actualizing your potential means you have to do the writing. Even if you find a ghost-writer and have a best-selling book published under your name, that still would not make you a writer—at least not in any meaningful sense. And the reason is precisely this: without doing the work and making the effort, you are unworthy of the name.

In O'Conner's readings of Kant and his successors, idleness stands in the way of our pursuit of worthiness: if we don't work hard to actualize our potential, we would be undeserving of the dignity that is proper to creatures like us. When it comes to work, then, the stakes are high because our life and identity are organized around it. What idleness threatens is not just productivity—it threatens our subjectivity, our very own sense of self. If we don't *do* things, we cannot *be*.

We will look at the relationship between doing and being in more detail in Chapter 7. What is noteworthy for the purpose of this chapter is that the stakes are similarly high in the pro-leisure writings[57] that we have covered so far. To quickly reiterate: for Tsui, rest and leisure are important because we need to work in a manner that is proper to our humanity (as opposed to working like a mere machine).[58] For Pieper, leisure frees us from total-work, thereby allowing us to live with dignity. For Shippen, reclaiming leisure is both a matter of political resistance and a necessary condition for self-actualization. For Lin, idleness has come to represent the honor of a high-minded intellectual who won't bow for fame and money. Similarly, for O'Conner, idleness rewrites our values as well as the kind of self that is proper to us. (Even though he contends that he is not promoting idleness.[59]) As such, our worthiness and dignity continue to be at stake in these anti-industriousness, pro-leisure writings. Whereas Kant and his successors believe that work is necessary for our worthiness, anti-industriousness thinkers insist that leisure or idleness is the key for us to achieve greatness (or, minimally, a state of being that befits creatures like us). In other words, pro-leisure thinkers continue to subscribe to the worthiness myth by appropriating it and rewriting it.[60]

In his book, O'Conner repeatedly highlights idleness's indifference to purpose. This emphasis is in part motivated by the worry that idleness could be misconstrued as a productivity-enhancing strategy. Idleness's indifference to purpose is supposed to make it more resistant to this co-optation. Yet, despite the recognition that idleness can be appropriated by pro-work rhetoric, it seems that O'Conner himself cannot resist instrumentalizing idleness in his own way.

Consider O'Conner's insistence that idleness presents an alternative way of thinking about freedom. Whereas Enlightenment thinkers understand freedom primarily in terms of rational self-determination (or freedom from our natural appetites), O'Conner depicts idle freedom as "an implicit resistance—to specific recommendations about how one ought to live: the need for progress, prestige, or success through work."[61] Idle freedom is the kind of freedom that can liberate us from the bondage of social pressure and expectations. O'Conner's claim is strikingly similar to Lin's diagnosis of the "high-minded" scholars who prioritize integrity over fame and fortune. By choosing an idle life, they too reject the socially mandated conception of success.

Yet, there is something peculiar (if not self-undermining) about idleness being a form of social rebellion. After all, it is difficult to see how idleness could still be understood as "purposeless," when it functions as a critical voice against the cult of productivity. Granted, not all idlers are dissidents critical of social norms, and a life of idleness is not necessarily a protest. An idler may be "protesting" without even knowing it. But it is important to remember that by O'Conner's *own account*, the critical aspect of idleness is not merely an inadvertent side effect. As mentioned, one of his tasks in the book is to present idleness as a reasonable lifestyle, a lifestyle that a rational creature like us can reasonably adopt. So, idleness is something that a rational agent may *choose* in accordance with their conception of a good life.[62] This sort of "choosing" need not involve a strict notion of autonomy whereby "we regulate our desires under principles that will […] give coherence across our actions."[63] Nevertheless, it is still a deliberate choice guided by its own "needs and commitments."[64] The "idle freedom" that O'Conner speaks of suggests that an idle lifestyle is not something that merely happens to an idler, as if the idler simply slips into it and is trapped in the realm of idleness; rather, idle freedom is a deliberate refusal.[65] In fact, O'Conner even goes so far as to suggest that idle freedom "comes closer than the classical notion of autonomy to meeting the conditions of self-direction."[66] Instead of the classical notion of freedom as the ability to overcome one's natural inclinations, idle freedom prioritizes setting one's own values. Authentic liberty, then, means refusing to bow to socially constructed and sanctioned values.

Given O'Conner's effort to present idleness as a more authentic form of freedom, a lifestyle that one could reasonably choose, I wonder why he insists that his argument is not meant to promote idleness. What are we supposed to do with the information that there is a more authentic form of freedom achievable by exercising our choice? Are we supposed to treat that as a value-neutral matter? Perhaps O'Conner is doing more than merely "[preventing] the philosophical case against idleness from having the last word," after all.

JOSH COHEN

As we have seen, for both pro-leisure and pro-work thinkers, the stakes are high because work has come to define who we are. When doing and being are linked, contesting the ethos of work inevitably challenges our values and identity. Or, as psychoanalyst Josh Cohen contends, "not working is at least as fundamental as working to who and what we are."[67] In *Not Working: Why We Have to Stop*, Cohen uses his work in the clinic to articulate four different types of "inertial" individuals: the burnout, the slob, the daydreamer, and the slacker.[68] For the purpose of this book, the last group is surely the most relevant. Cohen's understanding of slackers is, in some ways, similar to the kind of slackers that I am defending in this book. For example, Cohen speaks of the "indifference" and the "aimlessness" of slackers—qualities that I consider essential to slacking. However, for Cohen, the slacker's indifference is more than just being disinterested in productivity or socially sanctioned accomplishments. He goes so far as to argue that their apathy affects their *beliefs* as well. In Cohen's account, slackers are natural skeptics.[69] They don't commit themselves to particular ideologies, nor are they interested in opining or virtue-signaling. Their non-committal attitude toward ideologies and reluctance to have an opinion are particularly jarring in the age of Twitter wars and Facebook tirades. Not only are we supposed to have an opinion, we are also expected to share it publicly. In one particularly revelatory passage, Cohen writes, "In our social media landscape, opinion has become the currency and substance of our selfhood. The positions we publicize have become a way of affirming the reality of our existence to the world. We pontificate therefore we are."[70]

The pro-leisure thinkers that we have examined are primarily concerned with how work has come to dominate our existence—both in terms of the time we spend working, and how we have come to define ourselves exclusively by what we do. What Cohen adds to this conversation is the following: our publicized opinions and ideologies, like our work, are integral to the productivity culture and its concomitant effect on our identity. The pervasiveness of social media has given rise to "the conception of the human as a propositional animal, a being defined by his proclaimed beliefs and public actions."[71]

The emergence of social media "influencers" on Instagram, Facebook, and the blogosphere exemplifies the intricate connections among publicized opinions, productivity, and identity. As we know, influencers are regularly recruited by companies to advertise on their personal accounts. An influencer who is famous for her makeup videos may be courted by a cosmetics company to promote their brand during one of her tutorial videos for example. Some influencers get paid directly; others receive free products. Either way, influencers are being compensated for publicizing their opinions on the product.[72] The job of influencers revolves around maximizing productivity (as measured by numbers of followers, posts, and likes) and maintaining their brand (a particular identity manufactured by carefully curated posts). In short, their publicized opinion is a confirmation of their productivity, as well as identity.

While most of us are not influencers, the rise of social media means that few of us escape the expectation to publicize our opinions. From liking a post by a colleague to engaging in a full-on Twitter war with complete strangers, our publicized opinions have become the sum total of our online profile, which is how we are often known by others nowadays. Against the backdrop of this oversharing culture, Cohen argues that the slacker's apathy toward opinions can be understood as "a quiet resistance" to a conception of the self that is defined by one's opinions.[73] The slacker's silence is an act of defiance, as silence "encourages us to think about and experience ourselves as irreducible to the sum of what we do and opine, as creatures who, beyond any action or achievement, simply *are*."[74]

Like other pro-leisure thinkers, Cohen is presenting slacking (here in the form of an apathetic skeptic) as a protest against our hyper-productive, status-obsessed culture. As with O'Conner's rebellious idler above, this protest is not an unintended side effect of slacking. In the conclusion, Cohen considers the subtitle of his book— "Why we have to stop." He insists that to stop (in the intransitive sense) is a matter of "choice."[75] More specifically, it is "an assertion of autonomy, an invisible act of resistance against the tyranny of action."[76] Once again, anti-industriousness is linked to freedom. It is not freedom in the consumerist sense of having a wide selection of products to purchase, but an "interior freedom" (what I have been calling "existential freedom") that allows us to "discover what it is we might want to do and who we might want to be."[77]

PURPOSELESSNESS WITH AN AGENDA?

Wary of the ways leisure has been co-opted by capitalism, some of our thinkers have taken great lengths to remind us that leisure/idleness/slacking should not be instrumentalized. Pieper insists that leisure allows us to pursue knowledge "for its own sake;" O'Conner describes idleness as "drifting" and "purposeless"; while Cohen emphasizes the non-committal quality of slacking. However, a closer look at their accounts reveals just how difficult it is to present a justification for a life of inactivity without assigning some merit to it. As such, even though leisure is not to be instrumentalized as a tool for capitalist productivity in these accounts, it is still portrayed as *purposeful*.

So, what is this new purpose that anti-industriousness is supposed to achieve? The thread that I have been tracing in these six accounts is the purported existential significance of anti-industriousness. The leisure-versus-work debate is never just about the work, it is more importantly about who we are, and how we ought to *be*. Instead of thinking of ourselves first and foremost as productive, money-making laborers, our anti-industriousness thinkers argue that there is a more authentic mode of being, achievable if we are willing to adopt a leisurely/idle life. Evidently, this authentic mode of being has to do with freedom and autonomy. For Shippen, actualizing our human potential requires a "temporal autonomy" (afforded by leisure) where we can control our non-work time in a self-directed way, in contrast to the reductive freedom as freedom to consume under capitalism. For O'Conner, idleness represents a more authentic freedom: it is not freedom in the Kantian sense of rational self-determination, but freedom in the sense of being able to resist socially prescribed values and expectations. To be an authentic or autonomous being, we ought to be able to write our own story.

While I don't deny the liberatory potential of leisure/idleness, I doubt that a life of slothfulness is still "purposeless" when these thinkers connect it to the pursuit of humanity, authenticity, and freedom. If we follow Russell and Pieper, leisure might not be "practical" in the everyday sense, but it is certainly instrumental to the advance of civilization and culture. And as we have seen, Pieper insists that leisure is the mark of our humanity; it is what liberates us from the indignity of "total-work." Existential freedom is a prerequisite for being human. But as soon as our humanity or dignity is on the line, leisure is no longer value neutral. Quite the contrary, it becomes an imperative.

In light of such lofty pursuits of cultural and human flourishing, Russell's, Pieper's and Shippen's ideas of leisure are incompatible with the kind of slacking that I am defending in this book. The defining quality of slackers, as I understand them, is their apathy and indifference toward actualizing their potential. They don't care to make something of themselves. When slackers engage in leisurely activities, they don't engage in them in order to fulfill a particular vision of human flourishing. As I suggested earlier, many find slackers disappointing or infuriating because they don't care to actualize their potential. But if slackers feel no compulsion to better themselves, why would they feel the need to advance civilization or defend human dignity? It seems unlikely that leisure would ever present itself as an imperative for the kind of slackers that I am defending here.

Both O'Conner and Cohen are attuned to the importance of purposelessness in their defenses of idleness/slacking. And yet both of them end up making idleness/slacking an act of resistance. However, when slacking is deployed to resist the tyranny of our productivity culture, is it still purposeless?[78] I submit that a slacker who is apathetic to social expectations does not slack for the purpose of being a critical voice—they simply slack. If their slackerdom happens to offer any commentary on our over-striving culture, it is completely fortuitous. A slacker does not achieve slackerdom, they have slackerdom thrust upon them. After all, if someone is critical enough of the dominant culture to adopt an alternative lifestyle (much like the high-minded scholars Lin speaks of), can they really be *that* indifferent or apathetic to such a culture? It would seem that the opposite is true. That is, they would have to care enough about the social ills produced by our status-obsessed, hyper-productive culture, and then make a deliberate choice to resist them.

Slackers may very well be an inspiration for the wannabe slackers, as well as non-slackers who are nevertheless critical to the culture of hyper-productivity. Their indifference toward social expectations can be a refreshing reprieve from the rat-race work ethic that many find stressful and stifling. But their way of living—however inspirational and enviable for non-slackers—need not be portrayed as some ennobling attempt to safeguard human freedom and dignity. The liberatory quality of slacking is, in part, due to the fact that slackers don't feel compelled to answer to anyone. There is no higher calling to which they submit themselves. Therefore, it is particularly ironic to insist that slacking is meant to fulfill some kind of human destiny or authenticity. What, if not cynicism, could drive us to assign the ultimate purpose of life to a supposedly purposeless way of living? Slackers just slack. That's what they do.

I began this chapter with a description of the ways leisure has been instrumentalized by the corporate world to improve productivity. I then proceeded to examine six distinctive accounts of anti-industriousness. While they offer relevant critiques of the culture of hyper-productivity and its capitalist, neoliberal underpinnings, many of them continue to instrumentalize "not working." That is, they continue to frame leisure/idleness in terms of how it may serve our purposes.

Specifically, how it may help us become the authentic, digni-fied, autonomous individuals that we are meant to be. Yet, as long as slackers are characterized by their purposelessness, slacking resists instrumentalization. As such, turning slacking into a choice, an act of resistance, or a remedy to our subjuga-tion to work is a fantasy at best, and a self-defeating delusion at worst.

What Are the Different Types of Slackers?

2

In this chapter, we will encounter a variety of slackers. My goal is to show that slackerdom is not an all-or-nothing affair. Some of the examples here may resemble textbook slackers, others less so. There are different degrees of slackerdom. By this, I don't mean who's the laziest of all slackers, but the extent to which the slacker in question satisfies the conditions of slackerdom. I will begin with one end of the slacker spectrum, the pseudo-slackers. Pseudo-slackers are slackers who *profess* to be slackers, and yet they lack the qualities that are essential to being a slacker. In fact, many of them are hard-working, hyper-productive individuals by conventional standards. These pseudo-slackers include the self-flagellating slacker, the social slacker, and the faux slacker. Next, I will look at the performative slackers. Unlike pseudo-slackers, performative slackers have the hallmark of a typical slacker—they make little effort and only do the bare minimum. The distinguishing feature of performative slackers is that they use slacking to show off. For them, slacking is a means to elevate their social status. These performative slackers include the disingenuous slacker, the posh slacker, and the recalcitrant slacker. Finally, I will end the chapter with the counterculture slackers. In many ways, the counterculture slackers resemble textbook slackers: they live on the margins of society, unconcerned with conventional notions of success and accomplishment. For the counterculture slackers, slacking is a *chosen* lifestyle.

I should note that we will not see the other end of the slacker spectrum until the very end of the next chapter. While many individuals we encounter in this chapter exhibit qualities that are commonly attributed to slackers (not working, falling short of expectations, etc.), they *care too much* to be a full-fledged slacker. Whether they are proud or ashamed of their slackness, their emotional attachment to their slacker status means that they are not the bona fide slackers that they hope or fear to be.

To facilitate our assessment of various slackers, here's the definition of slackers that I proposed in the Introduction.

1) A slacker is an individual who is underachieving; that is, they do not live up to their potential. 2) The slacker's underachievement is typically a result of their lack of, or insufficient, effort. And 3) the slacker's lack of, or insufficient, effort stems from a sense of indifference to the social expectation of making oneself useful.

THE SELF-FLAGELLATING SLACKER

When I discussed my slacker project with friends and colleagues, the reaction that I often received was, "Oh, I am a slacker! You are writing about *me*." At first, I was taken aback by such a reaction. Why would anyone claim to be a slacker in a world that prizes productivity? Why would someone willingly take on such an unflattering label? But then it occurred to me that many of my self-proclaimed slacker friends and colleagues are in no way slackers by conventional standards. In fact, many of them are considered high-achieving individuals. As academics, most of them have doctorates or other professional degrees. Many hold academic positions with a demanding teaching load, and yet they somehow manage to produce an impressive résumé with a long list of publications and accomplishments. So why do they claim to be slackers? What do they really mean when they identify as such?

My typical response to their identification of slackerdom was to roll my eyes and swiftly deny them the slacker status. "You are being modest." I would say. Yet it has become clear to me that this is not simply a matter of false modesty. Rather, many of them *genuinely* believed that they were slackers, despite ample evidence to the contrary. When pressed, some of them would downplay their hard work by attributing their achievements to luck, savviness, or institutionalized advantages— "Yes, I do have this well-placed publication, but that's because I was lucky enough to know the editor and got invited to submit a piece." More often than not, they would respond along the lines of "I could have done more." They would tell me, "I could have finished this proposal if I didn't waste so much time Netflix-binging last semester," "I should have applied for this conference, but I was too lazy to write the application," or "I should have finished grading this pile of assignments over the weekend, but I just couldn't read another paper butchering Descartes." While the reasoning varies, what these responses share in common is that my slacker friends and colleagues believe that they have failed to meet certain expectations (either self- or other-imposed). They feel a deep sense of underachievement, even if their résumés say otherwise.

My self-proclaimed slacker friends and colleagues fulfill one important condition of slacking—the failure to fulfill expectations or potential. They know that they could have done more, but they have chosen indulgence or avoidance instead. It is perhaps the fact that they *knowingly* fail what is expected of them that makes them feel like a slacker. After all, they didn't have any legitimate excuse for their unfinished proposal, unwritten conference application, or ungraded papers. There was no family emergency or unexpected illness that could explain their delinquencies. They know better.

However, before we grant them their slacker status, it is important to see whether they are in fact "underachieving." While it might be true that these self-proclaimed slackers fail to check everything off their to-do lists and that they could have done more, it seems absurd to call someone with a professional degree, full teaching load, and a respectable résumé a slacker. We would have to stretch the meaning of "slacker" so far that it may become unrecognizable. As we know, the stakes are high with publication in academia because it affects hiring and tenure decisions. The high-achiever's sense of underachievement is likely a product of their overly ambitious agenda, fueled by a "shoot for the moon" attitude and the expectation to be productive in academia. As such, the sense of "underachievement" perceived by many may very well be distorted. (Admittedly, not all self-professed slackers are misguided. Some of them are indeed "underachievers" who are nevertheless self-aware enough to acknowledge their slacking. But at the moment we are primarily interested in pseudo-slackers.)

Yet there is something amiss in their admission of slacking. Namely, the quality of indifference is missing in the case of these high-achieving, self-flagellating slackers. Far from apathetic, many of them feel guilty or embarrassed about not having done more. However, a full-fledged slacker, as I maintain, does not care about disappointing others or themselves. A slacker's résumé might be short, but as long as they have done just enough, there is no inner drive to better themselves. Likewise, there is no self-reproach that comes with the disappointment of not having done more.

THE SOCIAL SLACKER

Unlike the high-achieving, self-flagellating slackers that we have seen above, some self-professed slackers are well aware that they are not slackers; they just pretend to be one. The reason for their pretense can be rather benign. For example, some may pretend to be slackers in order to fit in. Suppose you hang out with a group of slackers—you may not want to stick out or be made fun of because of your industriousness. So you claim to be a slacker to run with the pack. Much like a social smoker, a social slacker is merely trying to conform to the culture by slacking. A close cousin of the social slacker is the empathetic slacker. Empathetic slackers do not feel the need to impress their peers, nor do they feel the pressure to conform. Rather, they pretend to be slackers as a way to show solidarity. "United we slack" is their motto. Suppose you have an assignment due tomorrow and your slacker friend has been procrastinating—you may profess to be a slacker around your slacker friend, even though you have responsibly completed your work. You commiserate with your friend by acting like you two are on the same slacker boat. Such a pretense seems benign. Granted, it is rather patronizing; but empathetic slackers mostly just want to make their friends feel better. So I will put these good-natured slackers aside here. In the next section, I will focus primarily on pretend slackers with a more dubious motive—the faux slacker.

THE FAUX SLACKER

Faux slackers typically wear their slackness on their sleeves. They advertise their slackness because they want to appear effortless and nonchalant. Like self-flagellating slackers, faux slackers may very well be high-achieving individuals. Whereas a self-flagellating slacker is typically misguided in their identification with slackerdom, a faux slacker is deceptive. Faux slackers are hard workers, but they cover up their hard work. If you ask a faux slacker whether they have studied, they may say "Nah … I didn't study for the exam. I played *Call of Duty* all night." What the faux slacker seeks is rather like the style *sprezzatura*—a carefully cultivated skill that *appears* to be effortless. Baldassare Castiglione (1478–1529), an Italian writer during the Renaissance, uses the word *sprezzatura* in his *Book of the Courtier* to describe the graceful way a proper courtier carries himself in court. *Sprezzatura* is "a certain nonchalance which conceals all artistry and makes whatever one says or does seem uncontrived and effortless."[1] A good waiter, for example, can carry multiple dishes to the table in one go. An excellent waiter with *sprezzatura*, however, can carry multiple dishes and make it look easy. For Castiglione, making a difficult feat appear easy "excites the greatest wonder; whereas, in contrast, to labor at what one is doing […] shows an extreme lack of grace and causes everything, whatever its worth, to be discounted."[2] This perhaps explains why the faux slacker is eager to appear effortless. They are worried that, by admitting their hard work, their accomplishments would be "discounted" and appear less worthy. The faux slacker is worried that trying too hard would make them look desperate; and worse still, if their hard work doesn't pay off, they would look foolish.

Is it OK to be any of these pseudo-slackers? A self-flagellating slacker seems incapable of appreciating their effort and accomplishments. Instead of celebrating what they have achieved, they are fixated on the unchecked items on their to-do list. But their delusion makes them pitiful, rather than blameworthy. The social slacker succumbs to peer pressure in order to fit in, while the faux slacker covers up their hard work to appear effortless. Both of them are trying to be someone they are not. Being deceitful is certainly not OK, but what we find objectionable about the social and faux slackers really is the deceit, rather than the slacking.

The pseudo-slackers we have examined thus far are, in fact, hard-working and high achieving. Some of these self-proclaimed slackers feel as though they should have done more, while others conceal their efforts in order to fit in or to inflate their accomplishments. In what follows, we will be inching closer to the other end of the slacker spectrum: performative slackers. Performative slackers are typically unproductive; however, far from being embarrassed by their laziness, these performative slackers flaunt their slacking in order to show off their status.

THE DISINGENUOUS SLACKER

Not all slackers lie about their efforts. Some of them really do manage to do well without working hard for it. Instead of faking slackness, these lucky slackers flaunt it. They may do so by feigning embarrassment of their slackness. They may say, "Oh man, I was playing video games last night instead of reading for my classes. I am *such* a degenerate," or "Don't ask me how long I spent working on this presentation. I am so lazy it's embarrassing." But what they are really doing is trying to impress. While the disingenuous slacker does not lie about their efforts (or the lack thereof), there is still an element of insincerity in the way they flaunt their slackness. After all, they are not actually embarrassed about their laziness; they are proud of it. The subtext of their feigned embarrassment is that they don't need to work hard to succeed. So, what they *really* mean to say is something like, "I don't work hard, but I can still get an 'A' on my exam." The disingenuous slacker wants us to know that they can "afford" to slack off because they are smart or naturally talented. Indeed, emphasizing the ease and effortlessness of their accomplishments is a way to inflate the slacker's skill. We are all familiar with the boilerplate comment that teachers love to dole out during parent-teacher conferences, "your son has so much potential—if only he would apply himself." The alleged lack of effort inspires us to fantasize about the kind of accomplishment that the slacker *could have* achieved if they had worked harder. As Castiglione puts it, "onlookers believe that a man who performs well with so much facility must possess even greater skill than he does, and that if he took great pains and effort he would perform even better."[3] By stressing and flaunting their effortlessness, the disingenuous slacker tries to make their accomplishments appear more impressive.

The faux slacker and the disingenuous slacker both want to appear effortless. They boast about their accomplishments under the guise of self-deprecation. Are they really slackers? I think we can confidently say that faux slackers are not real slackers. After all, they are high-achieving and hard-working. They are simply pretending to be slackers to score some extra credit. The faux slackers may act like, or profess to be, slackers, but they are far from being indifferent to their slacking (in fact, they very much care about it).

The disingenuous slacker, however, is trickier. They are not pretending to be lazy—they *are* lazy. What they fake is not laziness itself but how they feel about being lazy (hence the disingenuousness). The disingenuous slackers are in fact hyperaware of their accomplishments. They may want others to think that they could have accomplished a lot more, but it is unlikely that they would consider themselves underachieving.

Indeed, the disingenuous slacker would be extremely disappointed if their accomplishment goes unnoticed. But as our working definition suggests, a key feature of slacking is one's indifference to achieving one's potential. And once again we see that the quality of indifference is missing in the disingenuous slacker. A textbook slacker is indifferent to their lack of achievement; they don't really care about being a disappointment. The disingenuous slackers, however, need to show off (or perform) so that they can be the envy of their peers.

THE POSH SLACKER

As we saw in Chapter 1, Russell critiques the uneven distribution of idleness between the rich and the poor. Idleness has long been the privilege of the leisure class. The rich, landowning aristocrats are able to devote their lives to lofty, leisurely activities by exploiting the industry of the masses. What Russell invokes here is something akin to the stereotype of the idle rich: individuals who live frivolously because they don't need to work for a living. As a matter of fact, the image of the idle rich is something that one could cultivate. In *Idleness*, O'Conner speaks of "mannered idleness," an idleness that is

[Carefully] pursued and designed to create an impression of effortless existence comfortably elevated above the unintelligible toils of the masses. In its ostentation it involves little or no weakening of a conventional social sense. It wants to be *seen and admired*.[4]

As discussed in Chapter 1, O'Conner is primarily interested in how idleness may liberate us from the pressure of conventional success. However, insofar as mannered idleness aims to impress, it is at the service of prestige and social approval. As such, it is ultimately unfit to be the emancipatory idleness that O'Conner seeks to defend.

The idle rich are a helpful reminder that slacking can be a symbol of social status. Accordingly, posh slackers are those who show off their wealth by asserting their slackness. For example, the posh slacker may humblebrag, "Ugh, I am *too lazy* to walk. Better call my chauffeur." Or as 1990s supermodel Linda Evangelista famously says of herself and other supermodels in an interview with *Vogue*, "We don't wake up for less than $10,000 a day."[5] On the internet, parading one's leisurely activities on social media is a typical way to flaunt wealth. For example, the Instagram account "Rich Kids of the Internet" is curated to showcase extravagant shopping sprees, private jet vacations, exotic pets, and posh parties.[6] In October 2018, the "flaunt your wealth" challenge went viral in China.[7] Well-off Chinese millennials rushed to pose for pictures of them falling face-down with luxury items (expensive watches, designer handbags, cash) scattered all around them. This meme (known as the "falling stars") is visually striking: rich kids are literally lying on the ground to show off their wealth.[8] The frivolity of such wealth-flexing challenges is especially appropriate. Slackers are often perceived as immature and irresponsible, and the frivolity of such wealth-flexing challenges only reinforces such perceptions. Indeed, it is not just their lack of willingness or necessity to work for a living that makes the idle rich idle. It is also the frivolous ways with which they deal with money that makes them idle. By flaunting slackness via frivolous activities, the posh slacker is showing off their wealth and privilege.

THE RECALCITRANT SLACKER

Slackers may brag about things other than wealth, such as rebelliousness. You might have met some "cool," rule-breaking slackers in your school. They don't turn in their assignments on time (if at all). They don't seem particularly concerned about getting into college or having a respectable career, and they are generally impervious to admonitions from authority figures. It may very well be the case that they really don't care about their future, but their ostentatious *display* of apathy is still meant to impress.

Consider, for example, the iconic slacker in the high school movie *Fast Times at Ridgemont High* (1982). The character Jeff Spicoli (played by Sean Penn) has many cultural markers of a slacker. When a schoolmate suggests that he should find a job, he responds, "What for?" A veteran stoner who cares little about school (with the exception of one biology lesson held in a morgue), Spicoli loves to break rules and challenge authority. In fact, the very first scene in which Spicoli is introduced shows the shirtless slacker flouting the dress code of a burger joint. Spicoli is particularly fond of aggravating the authoritarian history teacher, Mr. Hand (played by Ray Walston). Spicoli habitually comes to class late, and when he does come to class on time, he has a pizza delivered straight to the classroom, much to the chagrin of Mr. Hand.

Interestingly, most of his outrageous actions are done in the presence of an audience. And despite his perpetually dazed look, Spicoli is not oblivious to how he is perceived. When Mr. Hand gives a private lesson (as a punishment) in Spicoli's own home on the night of the graduation dance, Spicoli barely puts up a fight. At the end of the private lesson, he asked Mr. Hand if he had "a guy like him" every year, a guy of whom Mr. Hand would "make an example." This suggests that Spicoli is well aware of the exhibitionist nature of his interactions with Mr. Hand at school. For the recalcitrant slacker, "not caring" about school is like being shirtless in a restaurant, driving recklessly, or having pizzas delivered to the classroom—it is one of the many ways to demonstrate their rebellion.

Neither the posh slacker nor the recalcitrant slacker is a full-fledged slacker, despite the fact that they *are* unproductive (at least in a conventional way). This is so because they very much care about being "seen and admired," to borrow from O'Conner. And while they might be indifferent to their GPAs or job titles, they are attached to their slacker status. The slacker status is important to them because it is the source of validation and their identity.

Is it OK to be performative slackers? For performative slackers, slacking really is a means to show off. Disingenuous slackers flaunt their intelligence, posh slackers their social status, and recalcitrant slackers their rebelliousness. The performative slackers can certainly be irritating to be around. And despite their effort to appear superior, their need to impress betrays their insecurity. But once again, these performative slackers seem more pitiful than blameworthy. Their need for validation makes them pathetic, but they haven't really *wronged* anyone by flaunting their slackness.

The performative slacker slacks to impress. But not all rebellious slackers are navel-gazers who try to show off. In what follows, I will look at a group of slackers that bear a close resemblance to textbook slackers—at least on the surface. That is, these slackers really are rather unproductive by conventional standards. Unlike the high-achieving slackers, they don't have résumés to contradict their slacker label. Unlike the performative slackers, they are not trying to impress. Rather, slacking for them is a deliberate *choice*.

THE COUNTERCULTURE SLACKER

As we saw in Chapter 1, anti-industriousness can serve as a critical voice against our hyper-productive culture. Slacking may very well be a thoughtful, purposefully adopted lifestyle. One example of counterculture slackers that we have already seen is the "idle Chinese scholar." As noted in the previous chapter, there is a long tradition in Chinese literary circles where intellectuals relinquish their official titles and retreat to a simple life of gardening and poetry writing. Within the context of a highly conformist Confucius culture, giving up one's title is a performative rejection of what the mainstream academic culture stands for: prestige, fortune, political power. As a result, adopting the life of ease and idleness is often praised as "high-minded," and slacker scholars are revered rather than rebuked. Their refusal to participate in the civic life (for which their academic training is meant to prepare) is a deliberate, carefully considered choice.

For a more contemporary example, consider Richard Linklater's 1991 film *Slacker*. This cult-favorite follows a group of young, seemingly unambitious outcasts in Austin, Texas, over the course of a single day. Lacking a discernible plot, the film meanders from one character to another, from one conversation (or monologue) to the next. There is no conflict to be resolved, no climactic ending to be had. As each character only appears in one or two scenes, there is also no character development. On the surface, the film mirrors the drifting, purposeless life of a slacker. Just as a slacker lacks life goals, the film appears pointless. But its free-flowing structure is deceiving. Far from lacking purpose, slacking is understood—and presented as—a countercultural movement. The colorful group of slackers includes a woman peddling a Madonna pap smear, business-minded children trafficking stolen soda, an armed burglar befriending the man he tries to rob, a boy-friend refusing to go out because "it's like premeditated fun," and many others. Few (if any) of the characters have—or care about having—gainful employment. There is a palpable anti-job attitude throughout the film, an attitude made explicit in the following exchange:

Video interviewer: What do you do to earn a living?
Hitchhiker: You mean work? To hell with the kind of work you have to do to earn a living. All it does is fill the bellies of the pigs who exploit us. Hey. Look at me. I'm making it. I may live badly, but at least I don't have to work to do it […]
Video interviewer: Anything else you want to add?
Hitchhiker: Yeah, there is something else. To all you workers out there. Every single commodity you produce is a piece of your own death.[9]

It is almost as if the hitchhiker refuses to get a job on principle. He justifies his lack of employment as a stand against corporate capitalism, a refusal to be complicit in an exploitative system. The notion that slacking serves as social-political commentary is confirmed by the filmmaker. In one interview, director Linklater describes slackers as "aggressive nonpartici-pants in a system they don't see much point in."[10] The outcasts in the film are "intentionally outside society or at odds with what was expected of it."[11] The intentional, purposeful nature of slacking is encapsulated in one particularly memorable line from the film, "withdrawing in disgust is not the same thing as apathy." Dissenting—and removing oneself—from the mainstream of productivity culture requires thoughtfulness, commitment, and creative effort. (It takes a certain ingenuity and tenacity to peddle Madonna's pap smear.) Slacking as a form of protest is a highly motivated countercultural move, rather than mere laziness or indifference.

Linklater once described his time being a slacker as "a very productive period in [his] life."[12] Being a slacker and being productive are not at all mutually exclusive, for working (in the sense of gainful employment) is only one type of doing. Linklater insists that the slackers in his film are not doing nothing. They go to movies and bookstores, discuss politics and menstruation, create artwork and their own utopia. They may not work a nine-to-five office job, but they are doers and creators. What *Slacker* rejects is not productivity per se, but the kind of productivity that is at the service of corporate greed. The critical aspect of *Slacker* makes the film purposeful, despite its nonexistent plotline and meandering structure.

Is it OK to be a counterculture slacker? A counterculture slacker deliberately rejects capitalism and the cult of productivity. I struggle to see why it would be morally unacceptable to use slacking as a commentary on social ills. In fact, many of us may even find counterculture slackers admirable because they are willing to live by their principle. Yet, there is something ironic about being a counterculture slacker. When slacking itself becomes a cause, a commitment, an expression of creativity, is it really still slacking? We are now back to the question that animated Chapter 1. If slackers are understood to be aimless or noncommittal, it seems ill-advised to make them champions of a (or any) countercultural movement. It is not the case that the slacker has no political awareness, or that they are indifferent to injustice. What I am doubting is whether *slacking* itself can become an instrument of resistance if it is supposed to be purposeless. Even if we look past the contradiction of being an advocate for apathy, the question of whether Linklater's slackers satisfy our conditions for slackers lingers. As noted, what Linklater's slackers challenge is the mainstream culture of corporate, consumerist productivity. They may not be outputting spreadsheets or annual reports, but they spend their time producing ideas and forging connections (mostly via conversations). In other words, if we broaden our conception of productivity, Linklater's slackers might not be as unproductive as they seem. In fact, they might be even more productive than someone with a nine-to-five office job. For Linklater's slackers, productivity is not measured by how many sales one can make or how efficiently one can turn labor into profit; rather, it is measured by one's ability to think critically and live creatively.

Linklater's slackers do in many ways resemble a stereotypical slacker with their seemingly aimless life, and they are certainly closer to a textbook slacker than the pseudo-slackers and the performative slackers that we encountered above. Nevertheless, as soon as we turn slacking into a cause, we take away the purposelessness that defines slacking. Accordingly, the counterculture slacker is not, in fact, a full-fledged slacker. But if this were the case, then we have a bit of a problem here. If Linklater's slackers do not even qualify as full-fledged slackers, who would? We will find the answer toward the very end of Chapter 3. The group of slackers we will meet in Chapter 3 are the Hollywood slackers. I will examine several iconic slacker films and discuss how the slacker as a character trope is being used in different ways. As I will show, a full-fledged slacker is a Hollywood slacker without a cause.

Are Hollywood Slackers Full-Fledged Slackers?

3

In Chapter 2, we saw some examples of iconic Hollywood slackers: Spicoli from *Fast Times at Ridgemont High* and the assortment of slackers from Linklater's film. In this chapter, I will focus primarily on slackers as a character trope in Hollywood films. Hollywood slackers often resemble textbook slackers: they lack life purpose, are unmotivated to change themselves, and are generally indifferent to their slacker status. With some exceptions, the typical slacker character we see in Hollywood films is almost always a white man. While the age varies—he could be anywhere from a teenage boy to a middle-aged man—a slacker is rarely a child or an old man. He is typically of working age. (This is unsurprising since one way to show the laziness of the slacker character is for him to be not working—when he should have been.) The Hollywood slacker is often portrayed as lazy or parasitic. His favorite pastimes are watching TV and getting high on pot. His permanent residence is either his friend's couch or his parents' basement. Although a slacker is typically portrayed in an unflattering light, he can also be an anti-hero to whom the audience may relate. Given our fascination with Hollywood slackers, it is helpful to consider the ways in which the slacker character functions in Hollywood films. What is it that we, the viewers, are supposed to gain from the slacker character? What sort of character development do we see in Hollywood slackers? In what ways does the slacker character help develop the plot? What is the moral of the slacker's story?

HOLLYWOOD SLACKER: THE MAN-CHILD

Laziness is a symptom of the slacker's inability to act his age. He might look like a grown man, but he seems to be stuck at the age of a carefree teenager. The incongruence between the slacker's age and behaviors sometimes serves as comic relief. But more often than not, it is supposed to demonstrate the character's refusal to grow up and own the responsibilities that are appropriate to his age. That the slacker is an irresponsible man-child is evidenced by the slacker's predilection to date or pursue younger women. In *Dazed and Confused*, another film by *Slacker*'s director Linklater, Matthew McConaughey plays the slacker character David Wooderson. Like a typical slacker, Wooderson is a laid-back pothead who seems to lack direction or purpose in life. Despite having graduated from high school long ago, Wooderson continues to hang out with the high school crowd. He pursues and dates younger high school girls unabashedly, as he makes clear in an infamous line: "That's what I love about these high school girls, man. I get older; they stay the same age."[1] Although he is the "cool" guy, there is also a tinge of sadness to his arrested development. Similarly, in *Pineapple Express*, Seth Rogen plays Dale Denton, a process server who gets high at work, hangs out with his pot dealer, and dates a high school senior, Angie (played by Amber Heard). Though Dale is only a few years older than Angie, the generational difference is repeatedly invoked in the film, reminding the audience that there is something dubious about the match. Also consider *Scott Pilgrim vs. the World*, where the title character (played by Michael Cera) is a 22-year-old unemployed wannabe musician. Scott shares a flat—and a mattress—with his roommate (and occasionally his roommate's hook-ups). The audience would later learn that Scott is leeching off his roommate, who owns 95% of the belongings in the flat and is trying to get Scott to move out of his place. Despite having an abysmal living arrangement, Scott does not seem to care to move out, nor does he make an effort to find gainful employment. Once again, Scott's slacker status is reinforced by his choice of romantic interest. The very first line of the film is a voice-over of his friend asking incredulously, "Scott Pilgrim is dating a high-schooler?"[2] Thus, we learn in the very first scene of the film that Scott is dating a 17-year-old high school student, much to the disapproval of his friends and family.

The older man dating younger woman trope is common in Hollywood films. In some films, it is meant to show off the "success" of the man or the greediness of the woman (e.g., the "gold-digging trophy wife"). In other films, it establishes the sleaziness of the man or the naiveté of the woman. However, in slacker films, it is meant to exemplify the immaturity of the slacker character. The slacker man-child is someone who doesn't act his age or date a woman his age. Given this particular feature of the Hollywood slacker, a common storyline of the slacker character is about how he overcomes his slackerdom and turns into a productive, responsible individual.

THE REDEEMED SLACKER

The "redeemed slacker" theme is particularly evident in the film Knocked Up, where Seth Rogan once again plays the slacker, Ben Stone. Ben checks many boxes when it comes to being a slacker: he does not have a regular job as he lives off money he receives in compensation for an old injury. While he does do occasional work for a porn site, he prefers to get high with his other slacker friends. In the film, Ben hooks up with an aspiring entertainment broadcaster Alison Scott (played by Katherine Heigl), resulting in her pregnancy. The main plot of the film centers on the ups and downs of the couple's attempt to make their relationship work in preparation for parenthood. Predictably, the slacker is supposed to pull his life together and act responsibly, while the high-strung, sensible goody-goody woman is supposed to loosen up and live a little. Toward the end of the film, we see a complete transformation of Ben. He gets a proper, more respectable job, moves out of his friend's house, and insists on being at Alison's side when she gives birth. Slacker no longer, Ben is now a productive, responsible citizen ready for parenthood.

Another slacker film with a redemption theme is *Mac and Devin Go to High School*. Notably, this is one of the few films that feature people of color as slackers. Once again, we have a super senior, Mac (played implausibly by Snoop Dogg). Like a typical Hollywood slacker, Mac hangs out with the younger students and deal pots to them. The main plot of *Mac and Devin* involves Mac trying to finally graduate high school after 15 years. Mac flirts indiscriminately with both the younger students and the older faculty. In one particularly lewd scene, Mac coaches a much younger high school girl into smoking a massive joint in the Assistant Principal's office. Their overheard discussion is captured by the school's intercom and mistaken as a conversation about fellatio. In the film, Mac becomes motivated to finish high school when a new teacher tells him that she will only go out with him if he graduates. Mac teams up with valedictorian Devin (played by Wiz Khalifa) to try to get his grades up. It is difficult to gauge the success of Mac's transformation, as he continues to smoke and deal pot for the rest of the film. It would be a grave overstatement to say that Mac has transformed into a productive citizen in the conventional sense by the end of the film. But at the end of the day, it is Mac who saves the science project that Devin has been working on throughout the film. And Mac does end up achieving the necessary grades to graduate. So, while Mac might still be a pothead at the end of the film, at least he has become a pothead dealer *outside* of his high school. As Mac's ambition to graduate is motivated by the prospect of dating the new teacher, his graduation would also mean that he would finally date someone his age.

In yet another slacker film by Seth Rogen, *Zack and Miri Make a Porno* features a different slacker redemption project. The slackers in this film find greater purposes in life when they finally apply themselves to actualize their potential. The film's title captures its basic premise: after having their utilities cut off, Zack (played by Rogen) and his roommate Miri (played by Elizabeth Banks) try to get into the adult entertainment business to make some cash. In the process, Zack and Miri become invested in making pornography, as well as each other. Several characters in the film exhibit slacker qualities: instead of paying for the utility bills, Zack spends his last dollars on a sex toy. While Miri is marginally more responsible, she lacks a purpose in life—her biggest ambition is to bed her high school crush at a reunion party. Zack's co-worker at the coffee shop, Delaney (played by Craig Robinson), is more interested in getting a settlement from the post office with a disability lawsuit than coming to work.

Inspired by a porn star they meet during their high school reunion, Zack and Miri recruit a group of colorful characters to make their adult video. At that point, we begin to see some character transformation. For the first time, Zack and

Miri seem to have a purpose in life. From casting to making costumes, Zack and Miri work tirelessly to make their movie a success. Connected by their shared commitment to making porn, Zack and Miri also develop romantic feelings for each other. Even though the porn-making enterprise is initially a last resort to making ends meet, the transformation from slackers to productive citizens show Zack and Miri the significance of work—as well as love. Indeed, making pornography brings positive changes to other characters as well. Toward the end of the film, Delaney comments on the impact of Zack and Miri's project to the crew:

> You see, there was a time when I was just a bitter old fuck making coffees, and Stacey was just a lap dancer, and Barry and Bubbles didn't know each other [...] Then two people come along and showed us something we didn't know existed. A world of possibilities where plain old people just like us could do something special. Even if it's something as simple as filming people fucking.[3]

As we have seen, one important feature of slackerdom is the slacker's indifference at achieving their potential. With this in mind, Delaney's remarks (however tongue-in-cheek) are meant to conjure the trope of slacker redemption. Like Zack and Miri, members of the crew have also evolved by actualizing their previously hidden talents. Everybody has grown up. The shared lesson of *Knocked Up*, *Mac and Devin*, and *Zack and Miri* is that with the right motivation, even a slacker can turn things around. Parenthood instills a purpose in Ben's life, the prospect of dating his teacher gives Mac a reason to finally graduate, while making porn brings out the best of Zack, Miri, and their crew.

Yet not all slacker films feature character transformation or a journey of redemption. As we saw in Chapter 2, Linklater's *Slacker* presents a collection of seemingly unproductive social outcasts unapologetically. The film has no discernible plot or stable characters. It moves from one dialogue (or monologue) to another, so we learn only snippets of each slacker. One moment we see a man running over his mother, another moment we see a man berating capitalism. Since none of the slacker characters linger for more than two scenes, there is no character development—let alone redemption—to be had. For Linklater, it is not the individual slacker who needs redemption; rather, it is our status-obsessed, hyper-productive culture that demands correction. *Slacker*, then, functions as a commentary on social ills.

This is not to say, however, that a story of transformation and a commentary on social ills are mutually exclusive. In fact, the theme of redemption may very well serve as a social critique in slacker films. Consider, for example, *Office Space*, an iconic slacker film directed by Mike Judge. Unlike other Hollywood slackers (stoners who mooch off their parents), the main character, Peter (played by Ron Livingston), has a stable office job that he goes to begrudgingly. As a computer programmer, Peter has the most tedious job—he goes through thousands of lines of code in bank software to change the year from two digits to four digits (98–1998). He finds his job meaningless, his boss overbearing, and his coworkers obnoxious.

Despite having a stable job and being self-sufficient, Peter fits the bill of a Hollywood slacker. When his next-door neighbor Lawrence (played by Diedrich Bader) asks him what he would do if he had a million dollars and no longer needed to work, Peter responds, "I would relax, I would sit on my ass all day. I would do nothing."[4] To which Lawrence rejoins, "You don't need a million dollars to do nothing, man. Take a look at my cousin. He's broke and don't do shit."[5] After a hypnotherapeutic session, Peter reaches a state of complete relaxation, and he simply stops going to work. In fact, he doesn't even bother to quit his job. Quitting his job would mean that he *cares* enough to tell his boss about it. As he tells his love interest Joanna (played by Jennifer Aniston), he is "just gonna stop going."[6]

While Peter may appear lazy and irresponsible, the important quality that makes him a slacker is his lack of motivation. In his own words, "it's not that I am lazy, it's just that I just don't care."[7] In Chapter 1, I suggested that a slacker need not be irresponsible (though they can be). Rather, a slacker is someone who fails to achieve their potential. And just as importantly, a slacker is indifferent to their lack of achievements. Peter is a slacker insofar as he tries to do the bare minimum to get by, as well as the fact that he is completely transparent and comfortable about his lack of motivation. For example, when he interviews with the two consultants who are hired to help downsize the company, he confesses, "my real motivation— is not to be hassled. That and the fear of losing my job, but y'know […] it will only make someone work hard enough not to get fired."[8] Ironically, the two consultants determine that what Peter needs is *more* responsibility at work so he is properly motivated, and Peter receives a promotion as a result of the interview.

Another character who is accused of doing the bare minimum is Joanna, Peter's love interest. Joanna is a waitress at the restaurant, Chotchkie's. Like other waitstaff, Joanna is required to wear 15 pieces of "flair" (pins or buttons with various expressions or statements) as part of their uniforms.

Despite being compliant with the company's policy, Joanna is reprimanded by her boss, Stan, for not going above and beyond with her flair. Their exchange is revealing as much as it is entertaining:

Joanna: Ok. Ok, you want me to wear more?

Stan: Look. Joanna.

Joanna: Yeah.

Stan: People can get a cheeseburger anywhere, ok? They come to Chotchkie's for the atmosphere and the attitude. That's what the flair's about. It's about fun.

Joanna: Ok. So, more then?

Stan: Look, we want you to express yourself, ok? If you think the bare minimum is enough, then ok. But some people choose to wear more and we encourage that, ok? You do want to express yourself, don't you?[9]

Stan cares not just about the number, but also the "attitude" that underlies the pieces of flair that his waitstaff is willing to wear. He wants Joanna to wear more flair because she wants to and chooses to, not simply because she is made to do so. For Stan, these pieces of flair are both the proof of one's commitment to work and a means of self-expression. This brings us back to the triangular relationship of publicized opinions, productivity, and identity. As we saw in Chapter 1, publicized opinions and ideologies, like work, are integral to our productivity culture and its concomitant effect on our identities.[10] With the rise of social media, our identity is shaped by our "likes" and comments online, and our productivity is often measured by our social media presence. Similarly, Joanna is expected to use her pins and buttons to express who she is, and just as importantly, to demonstrate her commitment to work. As such, Joanna's indifference toward her flair represents a rejection of our two default modes of existence: opining and working.

At first glance, *Office Space* may not appear to follow a redemption story typical of slacker films—the tale of a lazy, irresponsible man-child who transforms into a productive citizen. In fact, Peter's trajectory seems to be the very reversal of such redemption narratives. At the beginning of the film, Peter dutifully braves the morning commute traffic to go to work every day, in the middle of the film, Peter stops coming to work, and at the end of the film, Peter completely abandons his profession as a software programmer to become a construction worker. When Peter's former colleagues stop by the construction site, asking if he needs help finding a job (as though being a construction worker is not a proper job), he flatly refuses. In the penultimate scene of the film, Peter is seen demolishing the office building where he used to work (the building is damaged after a disgruntled worker sets it ablaze). In other words, Peter's very last act in the film is literally taking down his workplace.

While *Office Space* may seem radically different from the reformation projects that we have seen in *Knocked Up*, *Mac and Devin*, or *Zack and Miri*, the theme of redemption remains. Peter the slacker is redeemed not by kowtowing to productivity culture, but by rejecting it. (Hence, he is a dissident slacker.) Recall in Chapter 1, I traced several accounts of pro-leisure, anti-industriousness writings. I argued that even though many thinkers insist that leisure is good for its own sake (i.e., leisure is not a means to promote productivity), they continue to ascribe a purpose to it. For Russell, Pieper, and Shippen, leisure is instrumental to the advance of civilization and human flourishing. For O'Conner and Cohen, idleness is an implicit, quiet resistance against productivity culture. For these thinkers, "not working" is a means to a more authentic, dignified, and autonomous way of living. In light of this, what *Office Space* offers is an alternate path to a good life—one that doesn't involve sitting in an office tediously modifying digits. Even though Peter has lost his job as a programmer, he appears to be happier and more fulfilled at the end of the film. As he remarks on his construction work, "This isn't so bad, huh? Making bucks, getting exercise, working outside."[11]As such, the slacker is redeemed not by becoming a motivated, productive citizen, but by embracing a different vision of a good life—one that doesn't subscribe to a typical model of success.

SLACKERS WITHOUT A CAUSE[12]

Another noteworthy slacker film that doesn't take the typical redemption route is the Coen brothers' *The Big Lebowski*. "The Dude" (played by Jeff Bridges) is one of the most celebrated slackers of all Hollywood films. The film begins with the voice-over of the narrator introducing the Dude, who the narrator describes as "a lazy man [...] and quite possibly the laziest in Los Angeles County."[13] On screen, we follow a tumbleweed drifting along the Los Angeles landscape aimlessly. The first time we see the Dude, he is checking the expiration date of a carton of half-and-half in a supermarket in his bathrobe, an outfit that befits his laid-back slacker persona. Later, the Dude gets mistaken for a millionaire who shares his last name and is beaten up by "thugs." Despite the physical assault, what seems to bother the Dude the most is the fact that one of the "thugs" urinated on his rug. After deliberating with his friend Walter (played by John Goodman), the Dude decides to confront the other Lebowski (the millionaire "Big" Lebowski) in the hope of getting compensated for the rug. The main event of the film is the kidnapping of Bunny (played by Tara Reid), the wife of the Big Lebowski (played by David Huddleston). The Dude agrees to deliver the ransom to the kidnappers for a fee. After Walter botches the delivery, the Dude gradually discovers that there are multiple stakeholders in the kidnapping and that everyone is scheming for the ransom money.

Despite having the same name, the contrast between the Big Lebowski and the Dude cannot be starker. The Big Lebowski is an industrious, award-winning philanthropist who rubs shoulders with politicians. He heads a charity called "Little Lebowski Urban Achievers." The purpose of the charity, according to the Big Lebowski's obsequious assistant Brandt (played by Philip Seymour Hoffman), is to fund "inner-city children of promise but without the [...] means for higher education."[14] The assistant's description of the charity can be read as a commentary on the Dude. Unlike the Big and the Little Lebowskis, the Dude is neither accomplished nor does he show any promise to be fulfilled. In their first meeting, the Big Lebowski berates the Dude for being lazy, screaming that he is just a bum looking for a handout (even though the Dude is only asking for a rug).

On paper, the film's portrayal of the Dude is not particularly flattering. Yet, the audience is supposed to be sympathetic to the Dude. Why is that the case? Perhaps it is just that the Dude is relatively harmless, compared with other characters. The Dude might be lazy, but he doesn't go out of his way to hurt others. He just wants to smoke a joint, go bowling with his friends, and drink his White Russians. Compared with his reckless, self-righteous friend Walter, who flashes his gun when slighted, the Dude looks like a pacifist. Compared with the manipulative Big Lebowski, who uses his wife's kidnapping as an opportunity to scam his own charity, the Dude looks like a caring guy (he is the only person who shows concern for Bunny's safety). And compared with Maude Lebowski (the Big Lebowski's daughter, played by Julianne Moore), who uses the unsuspecting Dude as a sperm donor without his consent, the Dude looks like an honest guy. In short, compared with most other characters, the Dude is actually a pretty decent person.

So what does that tell us? That there are worse people in the world than an apathetic slacker? Or that ambition might not be a good thing? Or that it is not so bad to be a slacker after all? *The Big Lebowski* has been analyzed extensively from different angles. Indeed, it has been scrutinized through such a wide-ranging lens that this film seems to be a commentary on just about everything. From its subversive fetishism[15] to its pedagogical value in an undergraduate class;[16] from its masculine underpinning to its mythic narrative,[17] *The Big Lebowski* seems to have something to say about all aspects of our culture. Yet, I hesitate to add a critique of productivity to the list. Unlike Linklater's *Slacker*, *The Big Lebowski* is not so clear with its intent to offer a critique on the productivity culture. The Dude is not slacking to make a stance; slacking is just what he does. Of course, a film can be *read* as a critique of society without the filmmakers' explicit say-so. But given the Dude's indifferent attitude toward life, it would seem rather ironic to read his slackerdom as some sort of manifesto. If the Dude offers any inspiration to wannabe slackers, it would be entirely accidental. As Walter points out, the Dude's answer to everything is a simple "Just take it easy, man."[18]

Like the Dude from *The Big Lebowski*, the characters in Kevin Smith's *Clerks* also appear to be slackers without a cause. *Clerks* tells the story of a day in the life of convenience store clerk

Dante (played by Brian O'Halloran), who has been called into work on his day off. Like Linklater's *Slacker*, *Clerks* also features a collection of colorful characters. We have the typical pothead slackers, Jay and Silent Bob (played by Jason Mewes and Kevin Smith). The duo are drug dealers who loiter near the convenience store. They steal food and antagonize Dante all day. We also have Randal (played by Jeff Anderson), a clerk working at the video rental store next door. Randal fits a typical slacker profile as he is lazy and irresponsible. He treats the store opening hours as mere suggestions, ignores his customers, sells cigarettes to a four-year-old, and regularly abandons his store to hang out with Dante.

Dante, the character who comes to work on his day off, offers a more interesting slacker case. Over the course of a single day, Dante closes the store twice: the first time so he can play a hockey game on the roof of the store, the second time so he can attend the wake of an ex-girlfriend whom he hadn't spoken to for two years. Skipping work to play a game or attend to personal business seems like a classic slacker move. However, for Dante (at least in his rationalization), playing hockey and attending the wake are actually "obligations." These obligations just happen to conflict with his duty as a clerk. After all, he has already promised others to play hockey on what he expected to be his day off. And unlike Randal, Dante does not attend the wake for fun—he attends it out of a sense of duty. In other words, even though Dante skirts his responsibility as a clerk, he does so in order to honor his other obligations, rather than simply to slack off.

Compared with Randal, Jay, and Silent Bob, Dante seems responsible. In fact, he repeatedly invokes a sense of responsibility in the film. For example, he chastises Randal for leaving the video store: "We are employees of Quick Stop Convenience and RST Video, respectively. As such, we have certain responsibilities which—though it may seem cruel and unusual—does include manning our posts until closing."[19] Nevertheless, Dante does exhibit an important quality of a slacker, which is the fact that he cares very little about actualizing his potential. This is evidenced by Dante's girlfriend's (Veronica) failed attempts at persuading Dante to leave his dead-end job and "get some direction."[20] In one scene, Veronica (played by Marilyn Ghigliotti) implores, "you have so much potential that just goes to waste in this pit. I wish you'd go back to school."[21] She even transferred to a college near Dante hoping that he would be more inclined to enroll again. Yet, Dante is decidedly unenthusiastic about the prospect of going back to school. He doesn't even bother to formulate an objection against going back to school; he simply doesn't *care* about it.

The theatrical version of *Clerks* ends with Randal leaving the convenience store and declaring to Dante, "You are closed."[22] The original version, however, ends with Dante getting shot and killed by a robber after Randal exits the store. While the original ending is certainly bleaker, neither ending suggests that Dante (or any other slacker character) has been transformed or redeemed. Dante is the same frustrated, unmotivated person to the very end. So, unlike *Knocked Up*, *Clerks* is not about transforming a slacker into a productive citizen. Unlike Peter in *Office Space*, the slackers in *Clerks* enjoy no luxury of self-discovery, nor do they gain contentment by embracing an alternative notion of success. Moreover, unlike *Office Space* and *Slacker*, *Clerks* does not offer dissident slackers, nor does it deliver any commentary on productivity culture. In *Office Space*, Peter finds contentment when he finally rejects a work ethic that is at the service of corporate productivity. In *Slacker*, the collection of social outcasts offers an anti-job counterculture that is leveled against corporate greed. As such, the slackers in these two films are a means to critique our conventional model of success. In *Clerks*, however, being a slacker is not an act of protest. Dante's lack of ambition is a product of his desire to stay in his comfort zone. Being unmotivated is just a more convenient way to live. While Randal may appear to be more rebellious, his lack of a work ethic is just a function of him being lazy and selfish. It is certainly not driven by an anti-corporate, anti-capitalist ideology. In the end, the slackers in *Clerks* are more similar to the Dude in *The Big Lebowski*: they are slackers without a cause. They all just want to "take it easy."

* * *

At the beginning of Chapter 2, I suggested that we view slackerdom as a continuum. Some slackers are merely self-proclaimed slackers; they are neither lazy nor low achieving by any conventional standard. These pseudo-slackers are on the farthest end of the slacker continuum. Some slackers are indeed unproductive or under-achieving, but they use slacking as a means to elevate their social status. These performative slackers are in the middle of the slacker continuum; for they are slackers in appearance, but not in spirit. Some slackers see slacking as a form of resistance. For them, not working is a protest against capitalism. These counterculture slackers are not quite full-fledged slackers because they are still, in a subverted way, invested in conventional measures of success and accomplishment. At least, they are invested enough to *reject* them.

The Hollywood slackers we encounter in this chapter are scattered across the continuum. Some Hollywood slackers are performative slackers, such as Spicoli from *Fast Times*; some are counterculture slackers, such as Peter from *Office Space*.

Some Hollywood slackers may have started out as a bona fide slacker (or pretty close to it), but they end up embracing the ethos of productivity. The full-fledged slackers, in my view, are the slackers without a cause. These slackers are not trying to make a stance with their slackerdom. There is no ideology behind their slacking, no moral to their story. The Dude from *The Big Lebowski* just wants to take it easy; he is not teaching us a lesson. Wooderson from *Dazed and Confused* is a sleazy slacker who just wants to hang out with the younger crowd and date high school girls. There is no redemption story with the Wooderson character, nor is there a grandiose speech criticizing the rat-race culture in which we live. And finally, we have Dante from *Clerks*. The pointlessness of Dante's slacker character is exemplified by his death in the original version of the film. Lest anyone is tempted to attribute some significance to the main character's death, the director Kevin Smith has confessed in an interview that he ended the film this way originally simply because he "didn't know how to end the movie."[23] In other words, the character is dead just so the director could wrap up the film. (Incidentally, the character Dante is based on the director himself, who had worked at six convenience stores in his youth.[24]) Could there be a more absurd—yet appropriate—reason to kill off a slacker character?

4

This chapter will focus on academic slackers: slacker students and slacker professors. As a college professor, academic slackers are particularly close to home. I regularly encounter them, occasionally worry that I am one of them, and I am endlessly fascinated by them. My personal investment aside, there are other reasons for devoting an entire chapter to academic slackers. First, slacker students are uniquely situated to showcase a key quality of slacking—the failure to live up to expectations. Unlike those in the workforce, slacker students are unpaid. Now, how can we call someone a slacker if they don't work for a paycheck? Slacker students offer an intuitive way to understand why we need to define slackers as those who fail to achieve their potential, rather than those who fail to perform their duties at work. Second, the stereotype of a slacker professor has a unique political relevance. As we will see, higher education has been under siege in recent years, and the stereotype of slacker professors has been weaponized by politicians to threaten or justify budget cuts. Few workplace slackers have this kind of political significance. Third, in addition to their uniqueness, academic slackers help us make sense of several common objections against slacking. For example, the objection that slackers are freeloading and irresponsible, or that slackers offend our sense of justice and fairness. A close examination of academic slackers sets the stage for entertaining such objections in subsequent chapters. Accordingly, even though there are slackers in every profession, I believe slackers in academia warrant an in-depth analysis on account of their uniqueness and relevance.

My main goal in this chapter is to paint a picture of what slackers in academia look like. I will discuss various reasons one may find slacker academics objectionable or infuriating; however, I will wait until the next two chapters to attempt a defense. I argue that procrastination and freeloading are neither the necessary nor sufficient conditions for being a slacker academic. Also, being fragrantly delinquent is not a sustainable way of being a slacker. So, while this may sound counterintuitive, a slacker academic actually has to be competent and somewhat responsible. A slacker student may skip some classes or miss a minor assignment, but they would show up for their midterms and dutifully turn in their mediocre final papers. Similarly, a slacker professor may not attend the graduation ceremony or show up during their office hours, but they would submit the final grades just in time to preempt scrutiny. The slacker professor may not be churning out publications, but they would publish just enough in some second-tier journals to qualify for tenure. The defining quality of an academic slacker, as I will show, is their lack of motivation to go beyond what is minimally required of them. They are perfectly content with being just "good enough."

SLACKER STUDENTS

What makes a student a slacker? We have seen several iterations of slacker students in previous chapters: Spicoli from *Fast Times at Ridgemont High*, who is permanently stoned; Mac from *Mac and Devin Go to Highschool*, who is primarily interested in dealing pot and dating his teacher; and Dante from *Clerks*, a college dropout whose lack of motivation to return to college is the main source of conflict between him and his girlfriend. While the pot-smoking super senior or college dropout is a recurring character in Hollywood slacker films, it is perhaps more representative of a caricature of a slacker student. The slacker students whom we encounter every day don't usually go to such an extreme. More often than not, slacking is associated with procrastinating. A slacker student may invoke the image of a high-schooler or an undergraduate who puts off their work until the very last minute. Whether a paper is due in a week or a month, a slacker student would wait until the night before the deadline to work on it.

Given that a slacker student is generally unmotivated to do schoolwork, procrastination often happens. Yet we should not conflate a slacker student with a procrastinator. For one thing, a slacker student may not procrastinate at all. They may even complete the assignment early because they put in very little effort or thought to it. For another, procrastination is often an emotional response to an unpleasant or daunting task.[1] A student may put off working on an assignment not because they don't care about it, but precisely the opposite. That is, a student can be so emotionally invested in the assignment that they become too anxious to do the work. For example, a student who is anxious about getting a bad grade and disappointing their parents may attach negative feelings (e.g., self-doubt, anxiety) to the assignment, thereby turning a low-stake assignment into a daunting task. But this particular breed of procrastinator does not really fit the profile of a slacker. After all, a procrastinating student who is anxious about the possibility of a bad grade is not at all apathetic to their academic achievements, but quite the opposite. Lacking this indifference or apathy to accomplishment, what we have here is a self-flagellating procrastinator, not a slacker.

Apart from procrastinating, a slacker student is often deemed irresponsible. There are many ways for a student to skirt their responsibility: not doing the assigned readings, turning in their papers late or not at all, freeloading in group projects, and so on. However, like procrastination, skirting one's responsibilities is just one of the many symptoms of slacking. Furthermore, like procrastination, there is a myriad of causes for a student to skirt responsibilities—being a slacker is just one of them. For instance, a freeloader may feel that others should do the work for him out of a sense of entitlement, rather than a lack of concern for his academic performance. Similarly, a student may be delinquent with their assignment due to poor time management or stress, and not because they are not invested in the course. If we follow the definition of slackers from the Introduction, then a slacker student is defined by a sense of apathy toward academic achievements. As such, while procrastination and a disregard for one's duty are common features of a slacker student, neither constitutes the defining quality of a slacker.

Who, then, is a slacker student? A slacker student is someone who does not live up to what is expected of them academically because they don't care enough to make an effort. While slacker students may very well be intelligent and able individuals, they are usually not academically inclined. That is, they don't find learning rewarding in and of itself. Despite having the aptitude to maintain a 4.0 GPA, a slacker student just wants to get by without trying too hard. As such, a quintessential slacker student is best described as someone who does just enough to get a passing or a "good enough" grade, someone who subscribes to the motto of "Cs get Degrees."

A slacker student is someone who lacks the motivation to do well academically. This perhaps explains why there is a plethora of research devoted to motivation in learning. One particularly relevant discussion is the distinction between intrinsic and extrinsic motivations.[2] A student is intrinsically motivated when they find learning rewarding in and of itself, whereas a student is extrinsically motivated when learning is simply a means to an end. Consider, for example, writing a research paper for a philosophy course. Jackie is intrinsically motivated while Sam is extrinsically motivated. Insofar as they are motivated, both Jackie and Sam would put in the effort to write the best paper they could. However, being extrinsically motivated, Sam works hard because he seeks validation from his parents. For Sam, writing a good paper and receiving a good grade are a means to an end. He is willing to make an effort on his paper even though he doesn't find the subject matter particularly interesting. In contrast, being intrinsically motivated, Jackie finds the work itself enjoyable. She finds the reading interesting and the process of research intellectually satisfying. In fact, even if Jackie does not end up receiving a good grade for her paper, she would still consider the learning experience valuable.[3]

The intrinsic/extrinsic distinction brings us back to Chapter 1, where Pieper argues that leisure is what enables us to pursue knowledge beyond the necessities of everyday life. Recall for Pieper, it is the freedom from the practical or the useful that gives us the freedom to seek knowledge for its own sake. It is this freedom from the mundane that gives us the liberty that defines the liberal arts. If we follow Pieper, then having leisure is essential for being intrinsically motivated. Ideally, college is supposed to afford such leisure—a dedicated stretch of time where students can focus on the pursuit of knowledge. Incoming freshmen are often told that they don't need to know what to major in right away, as a liberal arts education is meant to offer opportunities to explore their interests before committing to a major. A general education, then, offers students an opportunity to learn something for its own sake, that is, to experience what it means to be intrinsically motivated. The hope is that students select a major that they find intellectually satisfying, rather than merely professionally expedient.

Yet, with mounting college tuition, college students are justifiably concerned with their job prospects. With a crushing student debt always on the horizon, it is only reasonable for students to select courses and majors that they believe will help them get a decent-paying job. Majors with a dwindling job market (particularly in the humanities) are unlikely to sound attractive to students—even if they find the subject matter interesting. Of course, this is not to suggest that majors commonly deem practical (or "servile," to borrow from Pieper) cannot be sufficiently stimulating. It is certainly possible for students to find such majors exciting and intellectually satisfying. It is not uncommon for students to develop an interest in a subject matter that they didn't care about initially. However, when the question "what can I *do* with this major?" supersedes the question "what can I *learn* with this major?" it becomes all the more difficult for students to be intrinsically motivated to learn. Given the reality of higher education today, the kind of leisure that Pieper speaks of (i.e., freedom from everyday practical concerns) seems rather like a cluelessly privileged fantasy.

An intrinsically motivated student is likely to take the initiative to learn because they find the subject matter inherently valuable. What does this mean to a slacker student then? Given that a slacker student is defined by their apathy to actualize their academic potential, it is unlikely that they would be intrinsically motivated to learn. Nevertheless, even though a slacker student may not care to excel, they still need to do enough to get by. As a result, a slacker student is more likely to be extrinsically motivated. These external motivators differ in each case: for some, it might just be about passing the course; for others, it might be about keeping their parents happy. Accordingly, if a D is what it takes to pass the course, then that's the bar a slacker student would set for themselves. Or, if a B- is what it takes for the slacker student to placate their parents, then that's the grade for which a slacker student would aim.

One may wonder why a student slacker would still care enough to try to pass a course or to placate their parents. Why wouldn't a slacker student simply drop out? Even though a slacker is often associated with dropouts (such as Dante from *Clerks*), I think it is best not to include dropouts. For one thing, once a student drops out, they are no longer an *academic* slacker. They are just a generic slacker who used to be a student. Here, I am primarily interested in how slackers survive in an academic setting. For another, doing *some* work is often necessary for sustainable slacking. Recall in *Office Space*, our slacker protagonist Peter tells us that he is motivated to work only because he doesn't want to be hassled by his boss or to get fired. To be a sustainable slacker, Peter knows that he needs to be strategic about how much he slacks. If he fails to do his job, he will draw attention to himself, ensuring more work. The same holds true for the slacker student. Parents are more likely to intervene if their slacker child fails a course; they are less likely to police their child if they are merely getting a disappointing grade. So, a slacker student who wishes to slack in peace cannot be *too* delinquent.

Being a dropout is in fact counterproductive to slacking. Suppose the slacker student fails all their classes and ends up dropping out of college, what would they do next? Unless the slacker is independently wealthy, they would have to find a job to support themselves and pay back their student loan. Perhaps the slacker dropout would be lucky enough to get a slacker job with minimal work and maximal pay, enabling the slacker to continue their slacker way. But lacking a college degree, the more likely scenario is that the college dropout will have limited options when it comes to employment. It is more likely that they would end up with a standard nine-to-five job, which means at least 40 work hours per week. By contrast, a typical course load for a college student is four to five courses a semester. That's roughly 12 to 15 class hours per week. Suppose the slacker student spends an additional hour per class hour to study.[4] The number of hours the slacker would have to devote to as a student is still only 24 to 30 hours. So, even on the high end, the slacker student is working ten fewer hours than a college dropout. In other words, it is far more likely that the slacker has to work *more*, rather than less, once they have entered the workforce. As such, to be a sustainable slacker, a student (without a trust fund or the prospect of a magical slacker job) is better off doing minimal work to get by, rather than dropping out.

ARE SLACKER STUDENTS CAUSING HARM?

If Cs get degrees, why is there so much anxiety surrounding slacker students, especially in college? Why should anyone care if some students don't do their best? One answer is that being a slacker affects not just the student, but also those around them. Parents of slacker students are justifiably concerned with the future of their slacker children. After all, it is the *parents'* basement that the slacker student would return to if they drop out of college.[5] And if the parents are paying for tuition or co-signing the student loan, then they are also justifiably concerned with the return of their investment. For slacker students who rely on parental support, their lack of effort is not just a matter of disappointment; rather, their underachievement may affect their parents in a very material way.

A slacker student may affect others by depreciating the value of a college degree. Suppose we have two graduating seniors with the same major—one is a 4.0 student, and the other is barely graduating with a 1.7 GPA. While their GPAs set them apart, they are nevertheless receiving the same degree from the same university. As long as the slacker student made the required GPA to graduate, he is not undeserving. He did do what is *required*. And yet, it wouldn't seem unreasonable for the 4.0 student to feel that their degree is "cheapened" by the slacker. Consider the following: A professor is known for doling out easy As in their class. Getting an A from this professor would not be as meaningful as it would from a strict professor who is stingy with As. A diligent student may very well prefer to take a class that is more difficult to get an A in precisely because they want their accomplishment to mean something. By giving out As too generously, the professor has effectively depreciated the value of an A. Now, a slacker student who does just enough to graduate can produce a similar effect. If someone asked the 4.0 student and the slacker student where they received their degree, and in what major, they would give identical answers. Without reading the fine prints (i.e., their GPAs), the education and qualifications of the two students are virtually indistinguishable. It is not difficult to see why a 4.0 student may feel a sense of injustice when they are lumped together with a slacker.

Another common charge against slackers is that slackers are not contributing to society, or that they are freeloaders for not pulling their weight. In an academic context, a student slacker can certainly be a freeloader. Many of us know of students who did not contribute to a group project and still had the audacity to sign their name on the assignment. A parasitic slacker student does wrong to others by exploiting their labor, and they are also being dishonest by claiming credit that they have not earned.

I will say more about parasitic slackers in Chapter 5. For now, it is enough to point out that not all slackers are freeloaders. Someone who does just enough to earn a D in their class fits the bill of a slacker, even though they are not imposing a burden on, or taking advantage of, others. It is also difficult to see why getting an "A" in one's class is considered a contribution to society. It seems like an overstatement to call a student's calculus homework a "contribution" to our collective knowledge. What is a student supposed to contribute, or to produce, *as a student*? Under the regime of capitalism, productivity or contribution is often measured in economic terms. But being a student is not a job that one gets paid for—at least, not in a traditional sense where one exchanges one's labor for money. Some students may receive a scholarship, and they are expected to maintain a certain GPA in order to keep their funding. But even with scholarship students, the effort that they are expected to make is not an exchange of labor. In many cases, scholarship students are expected to maintain a certain GPA so that they are "worthy" of the honor of receiving a scholarship. They are not offering a service to their benefactors in exchange for payment.

Given that students are not expected to render services or products for their "job," nor do they get paid in exchange for their labor in a conventional sense, the slacker student is a rather unique breed of slackers. This, I believe, is why we need a definition of slackers that captures individuals who fall short of their potential, rather than irresponsible individuals who fail to do their fair share of work. Granted, contribution or productivity is not assessed in economic terms exclusively. One may contribute to the body of knowledge with a new discovery or a new way of thinking. Perhaps a student can contribute to the intellectual repository much like a professor is expected to. But for the most part, students are so to speak "in training." They are learning the ropes of their discipline. We don't expect them to write an opus magnum in their composition class, nor do we expect any groundbreaking discoveries in their chemistry lab class. What we expect from a student, then, is not so much the knowledge that they may impart, but more so the fulfillment of their individual potential. Accordingly, what is disappointing or troubling about a slacker student is that they fail to self-improve. Even if a slacker student is not freeloading or taking credit that they didn't earn, they still owe it to themselves to make something of themselves. It seems that, by being a slacker, a student has first and foremost wronged themselves, and not necessarily those around them. The idea that we have a duty to make something of ourselves deserves fuller treatment. But, for now, my goal is to offer a snapshot of academic slackers, and I will wait until Chapter 6 to further explore the idea of self-betterment.

SLACKER PROFESSORS

A different group of academic slackers is the slacker professor. Unlike a student, a professor does get paid. Unlike a student, a professor is not an apprentice in training. In fact, professors are very much expected to impart—and produce—knowledge. Despite the differing expectations, I submit that the defining quality of a slacker student also applies to a slacker professor. That is, what makes a professor a slacker is not so much about their delinquency, but rather their lack of motivation to go above and beyond what is required.

For those outside of academia, the life of a college professor often resembles the life of a slacker. For one thing, the tenure system seems particularly responsible for enabling slacker professors. The narrative goes something like this: given that the bar for revoking tenure is extremely high, tenured professors take advantage of their job security. Some abandon their research altogether, while others make little effort in teaching students or servicing their institution. Once professors receive the security of tenure, they no longer care.

For another, even pre-tenure, professors seem to have unusually short working hours. Suppose a professor teaches a regular 16-week semester twice a year, they are only teaching 32 weeks out of the year. While teaching loads vary, college professors typically spend between 9 and 15 hours a week in the classroom. And depending on how their classes are distributed, many of them come to campus only two to three times a week on their teaching days, effectively giving themselves a long weekend every week. Indeed, politicians have used the stereotype of a lazy professor to attack higher education. In 2015, Wisconsin Governor Scott Walker proposed a 300 million budget cut for higher education. He defended his proposal by invoking the stereotype of a lazy professor. He took a jab at university professors, saying that they "should start thinking about teaching more classes and doing more work."[6]

For those who are unfamiliar with academic life such as college dropout Governor Walker, the image of the lazy professor who is overpaid and underworked is perhaps excusable. Unfortunately, even those who should have known better propagate the lazy professor stereotype. In an opinion piece "Do College Professor Work Hard Enough?", long-time university administrator David C. Levy maintains that college professors are getting paid like an "upper-middle class professional" despite working substantially fewer hours.[7] Levy argues that the way to address the rising college cost is not to invest more public funding, but to reform "outmoded employment policies that overcompensate faculty for inefficient teaching schedules."[8]

Of course, once we look beyond the surface, those who give credence to the lazy professor stereotype are either ill-informed or willfully misleading. First, while there are certainly professors who just turned on the cruise-control after receiving tenure, they are not representative of the profession. There are individuals who know how to "game the system" in each profession. And the existence of lazy professors only shows that even institutions of higher education can be exploited. There are plenty of tenured professors who continue to be diligent and productive. Second, it is true that a professor does not spend 40 hours teaching in the classroom per week, but most of what a professor does actually happens outside the classroom. Professors have to prepare for classes, grade papers and exams, advise and mentor students, and perform services for the college—all the while trying to maintain an active research agenda.[9] In short, job security and flexible schedule notwithstanding, being a professor is not a cushy as it seems.

Aside from the atypical work schedule that gives a false impression of an underworked professor, there is another contributing factor to the lingering stereotype of lazy academics who have too much time on their hands. Ironically, the freedom that is at the very core of academic pursuit also inadvertently reinforces this problematic stereotype. Recall for Pieper, leisure affords us the opportunity to pursue knowledge for its own sake. (Or in today's parlance, to be intrinsically motivated to learn.) By "leisure," Pieper is referring not just to free time, but also the freedom from our everyday concerns for survival. After all, it is difficult to find the mental space for Socrates or Shakespeare if one has to worry about next month's rent or a broken car. Pieper is quite right to point out the incompatibility between our mundane concerns and the pursuit of knowledge for its own sake. Yet, there is a flip side to this idyllic academic world in which leisured professors devote their life to subject matters that seem far remote from the ordinary world. The image of Descartes sitting alone by the fire meditating on his own existence immortalizes the perception of an armchair academic.[10] In fact, a common charge against academics (especially in the humanities) is that they live in an ivory tower, detached from real-world issues and concerns. For many, academics engage in esoteric debates, use highly technical writing styles in their articles, and generally seem uninterested in making their work accessible to non-specialists. For these reasons, the production of knowledge or the exchange of ideas may not always seem tangible for non-academics.

Consider, for example, the discipline of philosophy. What does a philosophy professor do exactly? What is it that a philosopher *produces*? In a university setting, a philosophy professor teaches classes, so what they offer or produce is teaching as a service. But what else do they do? They publish books, review journal articles, give presentations at conferences, and so on. While most of us would like to believe that our work matters, from the perspective of a non-academic, it is understandably difficult to see the relevance of some abstruse philosophical quarrel on how to read a particular passage in Heidegger's *Being and Time*. The lack of relevance of, or the lack of concern for, the practical, in turn, reinforces the perception of a lazy academic. A philosopher may be churning out page after page, book after book, but being prolific doesn't necessarily mean being productive (in the sense of being significant or functional) in the eyes of those outside of academia. All this is not to suggest there is no value in recondite academic research, and it is not the job of a professor to produce crowd-pleasers. What I am offering here is diagnostic—there are reasons why the stereotype of a lazy professor lingers.

In light of the malignant stereotype of a lazy professor, it is rather ironic that so many of my colleagues in academia profess to be a slacker. In Chapter 2, I introduced the category of "high-achieving, self-flagellating" pseudo-slackers. Many of my colleagues in academia identify as a slacker, even though their impressive résumés suggest otherwise. These self-flagellating slacker professors are not being disingenuous, as they genuinely feel a sense of underachievement. They know that they could have spent their winter break working on an article, but they have chosen to binge on Netflix instead. But as I argued there, even though they may not have checked off every item on their to-do list, these high-achieving professors are far from being indifferent to their academic accomplishments.[11] In fact, their angst suggests that the opposite is the case. The very fact that they are bothered by their "laziness" shows that they are not the slacker they claim (or fear) to be.

So who counts as a slacker professor? Perhaps we can start with the freeloaders. Just as there are freeloading students in a group project, there are freeloading professors in collaborative projects. While in the humanities single-authored publication is still the norm, in many disciplines (especially in the sciences and the social sciences), multi-authored publication has become the standard. This gives rise to the issue of inappropriate authorship attribution.[12] The order of authorship in a journal article is supposed to reflect the contribution of each author, allowing the author to be recognized accordingly. After all, it seems unjust for the co-author who did minimal work to receive the same level of recognition as other co-authors who made substantial contributions to the project. Yet it is not always easy to negotiate the order of authorship.[13] One author curated the data; the other author developed the methodology—whose name should come first? One author conceptualized the project and designed the experiment; the other author wrote the bulk of the paper—whose contribution is more significant? While the first author is typically reserved for the individual who is principally responsible for the project, the difference between, say, the fifth and the sixth authors is not necessarily obvious.[14]

To make the matter worse, there is the issue of "gift authorship" or "honorary authorship," where an individual is credited as one of the authors even though they did not make a substantial (or any) contribution to the paper. Sometimes, an "honorary" author may not even know that they were "gifted" authorship until the publication comes out, so the "freeloading" scholar is not necessarily at fault. To address the issue of inappropriate author attribution, many journals now require a detailed account of each co-author's contribution to the submission. Some journals even offer specific criteria for authorship in order to prevent dishonest author attribution.[15]

In addition to freeloading on the research front, a professor may slack off by coming to class late, not returning assignments, substituting lectures with YouTube videos, canceling classes for trivial reasons, missing department or other committee meetings, and so on.[16] Nevertheless, I think the best way to understand a slacker professor is not by citing their delinquent behaviors, for I believe their delinquencies are merely symptoms of their slacking. Rather, much like a slacker student, a slacker professor strives to be "good enough." Like a slacker student, a slacker professor merely wants to get by. The defining feature of a slacker professor, then, is their lack of motivation to achieve their academic potential professionally. They could have done more as an academic, but they would rather take it easy.

If "good enough" for a slacker student means reaching the bare minimum of GPA to graduate, "good enough" for a slacker professor means getting tenure. As we know, there are three main areas of duty a typical tenured/tenure-track professor is expected to perform: research, service, and teaching. If three articles are sufficient for tenure, a slacker professor would not bother to publish (or write) the fourth. If serving on two committees is good enough for the service requirement, a slacker professor would not volunteer for the third. If offering classes is the only stated duty, a slacker professor wouldn't go out of their way to mentor or advise students outside of the classroom. And finally, as long as the institution they work for is good enough, a slacker professor lacks the ambition to seek a more prestigious job elsewhere. After all, applying for jobs is a lot of work!

The distinction between intrinsic and extrinsic motivations is once again relevant here. A slacker professor is typically extrinsically motivated: they'd keep a research agenda because this is what it takes to get tenure, they'd teach their classes well enough because they need some decent teaching evaluations, and they attend campus events because they need to be seen by the right people. Publishing a paper, giving a talk, or going to a student-led theater production is not an end in and of itself; mostly, these are just items that the slacker professor can now check off their to-do list. Just as a slacker student is apathetic to their academic accomplishment, a slacker professor does not see being a scholar/professor as their calling. They might have become an academic simply because it was the path of least resistance. Or they might have been passionate about their profession or discipline at one point but have now become cynical and jaded. Regardless of how their slackerdom is inaugurated, slacker professors find little intrinsic value in what they do.

ARE SLACKER PROFESSORS CAUSING HARM?

Why do we find slacker professors objectionable? Is it just that the slacker professor is not doing their job? As mentioned, unlike a slacker student, a professor does get paid for their services. A professor has duties to research, teach, and perform services. A slacker professor is not doing right by their students if they are offering substandard classes, and they are not doing right by their colleagues and institution if they are not pulling their weight. But once again, being irresponsible is just a common, but not a necessary, condition of being a slacker professor. In fact, most slacker professors cannot be too irresponsible, for failing to do one's job is not conducive to being a slacker professor. As we know, doing some work—enough work—is necessary for sustainable slacking. A slacker student has to do enough work to pass their courses and maintain their GPA. Falling short of that, they risk interference from their parents. Similarly, if a slacker professor is too irresponsible, they risk drawing scrutiny from their chair, to whom their students and colleagues may have registered complaints. So, at least for strategic reasons, the slacker professor cannot be outrageously irresponsible.

If, as I argue, being a slacker means doing "just enough" to get by, and that being a slacker professor does not necessarily mean being an irresponsible instructor or colleague, then why should we be bothered by them? Why should we be bothered by the slacker professor's apathetic attitude—as long as they still deliver? In the case of a slacker student, we lament the wasted promise, and the missed opportunity to engage in intrinsic learning. In the case of a slacker professor who does minimal research and publication, we may also lament the potential loss in the production of knowledge. But I think there is also something unique about the profession of college educator that makes a slacker professor particularly troubling.

First, there is a social expectation for educators to be role models. Professors are supposed to teach by example and be "inspirational." (A caring, exceptional professor may even change the life of a student. Professor Keating from *Dead Poets Society* is one such example.) Given the extensive research on motivational learning, there is no shortage of pedagogical advice geared toward properly motivating students. It is not enough for professors to motivate their students with sticks and carrots, they are expected to motivate them the right way—to help them see the value of learning beyond a good grade or other external validation. If professors are expected to inspire and motivate, then slacker professors present a problem: how could a slacker professor make a case for the intrinsic value of learning if they don't even see the intrinsic value of teaching themselves? How could a professor inspire others when they lack enthusiasm in what they do? The slacker professor's apathetic attitude seems incompatible with the model of motivational learning that dominates education. Indeed, if learning happens in part through emulation, then a slacker professor who strives to be "just good enough" serves a rather questionable model. Even if the slacker professor is willing to talk the talk, their apathetic attitude and behaviors may speak louder than their words.

Second, we may find a slacker professor objectionable because they offend our sense of fairness. As I argued above, a 4.0 student may feel like their degree is "cheapened" if a slacker who does the bare minimum is also receiving the same degree. The same applies to professors seeking a promotion. Suppose two junior professors are going up for tenure in the same institution—a go-getter and a slacker. The go-getter professor does above and beyond: publishing more articles than required, serving on more committees than expected, and mentoring more students than any of their colleagues. Meanwhile, the slacker professor does the absolute minimum required for tenure. It is not difficult to imagine the sense of unfairness and resentment that the go-getter professor may feel if both of them receive tenure. It is not so much that the slacker professor is undeserving (they have done what is required after all), but that the two of them are rewarded in the same way even though the go-getter has clearly done a lot more work. It seems unjust that the two should have received the same credit and compensation given the disparity in their labor and accomplishments.

Third, at a university, no good deed goes unpunished. The go-getter's effort may be "recognized" in the worst possible way by having more work piled on them. Other faculty colleagues are naturally more inclined to think of the go-getter professor when they need a favor. Students are more likely to ask the go-getter professor for advice or mentorship.

Meanwhile, by laying low, the slacker professor is more likely to avoid unwanted tasks. While winning the goodwill of others can be beneficial (some go-getters may even find it satisfying in and of itself), it does not take away the fact that there is an uneven distribution of work. By being obliging and capable, the go-getter professor may find themselves constantly drowning in committee or mentoring work, while the slacker professor is being rewarded with a lighter workload for doing nothing. Of course, one may argue that as long as the added work is "above and beyond," the go-getter can always decline. But even if this were the case, the go-getter professor is still shouldering a disproportionate burden to decline requests from colleagues and students, as well as the resultant guilt of having to disappoint them.

There is yet another way a slacker professor may offend our sense of justice. That is, they are taking up a job that could have gone to a more deserving individual. Given the dwindling academic job market, slacker professors are especially infuriating to those unemployed academics who are actually willing to contribute to the field and institution. It seems especially unfair when diligent, productive scholars are struggling in adjunct hell while slacker professors are basking in the tenure idyll.

Finally, there is the issue of collegiality. As I mentioned, college professors already have the reputation of being underworked and overpaid. The slacker professors seem to be doing a disservice to their fellow academics by perpetuating the very stereotype that the non-slackers are trying to combat. Slacker professors are the "bad apples" who are nevertheless cited as the norm of the profession. They are professors who give academics a bad name. Given that the stereotype of a lazy professor has been used to defend budget cuts in universities, it is not an overstatement to say that a slacker professor is threatening the very future of higher education.

So, where does this leave us? Is doing the bare minimum actually not enough for a professor? Is it, in fact, not OK to be a slacker professor, given the sense of injustice that they invoke? These are matters I will return to in the next two chapters.

5

In Chapter 4, we looked at two types of slacker academics: the slacker student and the slacker professor. While I identified several objections to slacking in the academic context, I have yet to address them. So, in this and the next chapters, I will mount a defense of slackers by responding to some of the common charges of which slackers are supposedly guilty. This chapter will focus on third-party harm. That is, the harm that a slacker may do to others. We will look at three objections related to third-party harm: first, slackers take advantage of other people (i.e., freeloading); second, slackers "game the system"; and third, slackers impose emotional distress on others.

SLACKERS ARE FREELOADING

One objection to slacking is that slackers are parasitic, or freeloading. And freeloaders impose undue burdens onto others. For example, consider the slacker student who refuses to do their share of work in a group project or the slacker student who drops out of college and leaves their parents with substantial debt. Perhaps what makes a freeloading slacker especially infuriating is their indifferent attitude. They seem to have a complete lack of regard for those around them, be they groupmates or parents.

Admittedly, a parasitic slacker who cares little about others is difficult to defend. It is surely not OK for a slacker to impose burdens on others just because they can't bring themselves to care. Yet, are all slackers freeloaders? Are slackers always parasitic? As we saw in Chapter 4, students or professors who do just enough to get by count as slackers, even if they are not freeloading on anyone. If we insist on including "freeloading" or "parasitic" in our definition of a slacker, we risk having a definition that is too narrow. We would exclude slacker students and professors who do what they are asked but are completely unmotivated to go above and beyond. A definition that requires slackers to be freeloading would also exclude individuals like the "Dude" from *The Big Lebowski*, who is the paragon of the Hollywood slacker. As we saw in Chapter 3, the Dude's slackerdom is exemplified by his apathetic attitude toward the world around him, not any freeloading. The Dude didn't ask for a handout from The Big Lebowski; all he wanted was a rug to replace the one the "thugs" had soiled. Indeed, much of the film revolves around the Dude trying to accomplish a mission—delivering a ransom. Granted, he failed at that mission, but mostly due to his friend's interference and not for lack of trying. It doesn't seem quite right to describe the Dude as irresponsible, freeloading, or parasitic. He is a slacker who simply doesn't care to make something of himself.

A related objection to slacking is that a slacker is irresponsible. The idea is that since a slacker doesn't care about being accomplished, they are unmotivated to do their job. For example, a slacker student who does not care about their academic achievement may not turn in their assignments, or if they are in a group project, they would just let other students pick up their slack. However, the fact that a slacker lacks ambition doesn't mean they won't do what is minimally required of them. Plenty of people find their jobs meaningless or even detestable, yet they still manage to do what needs to be done. In fact, doing the bare minimum in order to avoid scrutiny from others is a practical strategy for slackers. As Peter from *Office Space* tells us, he does just enough to get by so his boss leaves him alone. Similarly, a slacker student is more likely to turn in a mediocre paper just so they can pass the course rather than taking the trouble to retake it, and they may rather do their share of the group work than having to deal with complaints from others. Indeed, just as indifference doesn't necessarily translate into delinquency, enthusiasm is not a guarantee of accountability. Caring too much about one's work can be anxiety-inducing. In other words, interest in, or commitment to, your job is not always indicative of how likely you are to do the work. In short, it is perfectly conceivable to have a slacker who doesn't care, yet still manages to do their job without being a freeloader or a burden to others.

Given that being a freeloader is an incidental, rather than essential, quality of a slacker, what do we actually find objectionable about a parasitic slacker? Is it really the slacking that bothers us? Or is it something else? What is it about not doing one's job that we find morally bad? It is certainly infuriating when your slacker groupmate refuses to do their share of work, resulting in an unfair distribution of labor. Similarly, it is maddening to have to pick up your co-worker's slack simply because they don't care enough to do what is expected of them. But in these cases, I submit that what we find objectionable really is the slacker's sense of entitlement. Thus, what may at first glance sound like an objection to slackerdom is in fact an objection to something else entirely.

The slacker's entitled attitude is probably why many of them are also considered "assholes." In *Assholes: A Theory*, philosopher Aaron James seeks to solve the puzzle of why so many of us are infuriated by assholes. He stipulates that an asshole is someone who allows himself to enjoy special advantages out of an entrenched sense of entitlement.[1] An asshole believes that normal rules don't apply to him because he is special—he *deserves* to be given special treatments. These "special treatments," for the most part, are rather insignificant. For example, cutting in line or interrupting a conversation. It seems fitting to call someone who commits minor social offenses an asshole. By contrast, it seems woefully inadequate to call someone who commits egregious crimes an asshole.[2] The guy who cuts in front of you at the grocery store is an asshole; the tyrant who commits genocide warrants a different term of condemnation. Given that the offenses committed by an asshole are typically minor, the inconveniences they impose are relatively minor as well. Accordingly, James argues that what actually bothers us is not the fact that we have to wait for an extra three minutes in line or that we have to wait for our next turn to speak. What we find bothersome, according to James, is the fact that the asshole fails to recognize us as his moral equals.[3] Most of us recognize the need to observe interpersonal norms that are necessary for a cooperative society (such as being punctual, picking up after yourself, turning off your phone during a performance, and so on). We believe that such rules apply to everyone in normal circumstances. An asshole, however, believes that rules that apply to other people don't apply to him because he is special. As such, he fails to treat others as his moral equals.

Following James, I suggest that what bothers us about our slacker co-worker or our slacker groupmate is not so much the extra work we may have to pick up due to their slacking. (Though of course, we are likely to find the extra work burdensome.) What bothers us is the slacker's entitlement—their failure to recognize us as their moral equals. When we are made to pick up someone's slack, we feel used. It is a sense of unfairness that troubles us. It is the injustice that we wish to protest. Yet, if this is the case, then what troubles us about a parasitic slacker is really the *parasitic* aspect, rather than the slacking.

SLACKERS ARE "GAMING THE SYSTEM"

In Chapter 4, we discussed the sense of injustice that a 4.0 student or a go-getter professor may feel when they are being recognized in the same way as their slacker cohorts. The 4.0 student is graduating with the same degree, from the same university, as a slacker student in their major. The go-getter professor is receiving the same promotion (tenure) as their slacker colleague. In both cases, the go-getter feels that their slacker cohort "cheapens" their accomplishment. In both cases, we see an unequal contribution of labor. Perhaps it is this aspect of slackerdom that people find objectionable. It is not that slackers are parasitic freeloaders, but rather that they achieve the same recognition for a lesser amount of work that grinds our gears.

Admittedly, the unequal contribution of labor strikes me as unfair. I agree that the go-getter deserves greater recognition than the slacker. And the go-getter's feeling that their accomplishment is devalued by slackers is also understandable. However, should we blame the slacker for this inequity in labor? The source of the inequity is structural rather than individual. The fact that a go-getter receives the same recognition as a slacker is a result of how the system of recognition is designed. Blaming the slackers is a misplacement of responsibility. Consider an example from Chapter 4: a professor who gives easy As. It is true that some students would not have earned an A from the course had the professor been more rigorous. But this does not mean that the students are the ones "cheapening" the As. Rather, the *professor* is responsible for the grade inflation, and hence responsible for depreciating the As. The students who wouldn't otherwise have got an A are beneficiaries of the grade inflation. At most, we can say that such students are not in fact deserving of the A. But we would be misplacing the blame if we insist that the "undeserving" students are responsible for "cheapening" the A.

Like the "undeserving" students in the example, the slacker student and the slacker professor are no doubt beneficiaries of a system where one's recognition is not always proportionate to one's accomplishment and effort. Though unlike the "undeserving" students, slacker academics are not undeserving as long as the system of recognition has not lowered its standard artificially to accommodate the slackers. As long as the slackers meet the threshold of success, be it graduation or tenure, they are not undeserving. The fact that they have not done as much as their go-getter peers should not count against them. (Not accomplishing as much as they could have potentially achieved is an issue we will consider in Chapter 6.) Indeed, even in the case where the threshold of success is too low—even if we believe that the standard being set is embarrassingly lax—the slackers are merely symptoms of the problematic standard. In other words, the slacker academics *expose*, rather than cause, a design flaw in how recognition is conferred in academia.

Another concern regarding the unequal distribution of labor is that the go-getter professors are often "recognized" by having more committee and mentoring work piled on them, and the slacker professors are "rewarded" with a lighter workload by staying under the radar. (I am referring to work that a faculty member performs voluntarily on top of their required tasks on the basis of their goodwill.) The disparity in workload is indeed unfair. But once again, we have to be careful not to misplace the blame. It is true that slackers are not carrying a burden comparable to the go-getters. But instead of blaming slackers for not stepping up, colleagues—especially those in the position to make referrals or assign tasks—ought to be more cognizant of the unequal distribution of labor when they ask for favors. For example, the chair of a department should keep tabs on each faculty member's contribution to the department and the university at large in order to equalize workload. If the university is looking for a faculty member from a certain department to join a committee or give a lecture, the chair of that department should consider recommending the slacker faculty first, rather than the go-getter. Of course, the slacker professor may turn down the request, but at least they are now the one who has to carry the unpleasant burden of declining and disappointing their colleagues.[4] We have to remember that our slacker colleagues are not incompetent or irresponsible; they just don't care to go above and beyond. Still, it falls not to slackers but to individuals in the position to allocate tasks to ensure a fair distribution of labor.

But what about the fact that there are many non-slacker academics out there longing to get a tenure-track position or even just a stable full-time job? Aren't they more deserving of an academic position than a slacker professor? Isn't it unfair that diligent academics are struggling to get a faculty position, while slacker professors are doing the bare minimum to get by? I do agree that there is something troubling about this picture. It offends our sense of justice when harder-working, deserving individuals are not faring nearly as well as the slackers. However, this objection merits the same reply to the problem discussed above—the slackers are *exposing*, rather than causing, institutional issues in academia. These institutional issues include: the overproduction of PhDs relative to the demand of the academic job market; the adjunctification of higher education, wherein administrators cut costs by hiring contingent instead of tenure-track faculty; and the reality that hiring and tenure decisions are not always made based on one's accomplishments and commitment (but rather on one's "fit" with the culture of the department). Just as with tenure, where our system of recognition fails to reflect the differences between a go-getter and a slacker, academic hiring does not always favor the most accomplished or committed individuals.

It is indeed extremely problematic that many deserving academics are left in the cold. But as fellow academics, we fail them with our indifference to their plight, not with our slacking. A go-getter professor who is unconcerned about the institutional injustice their adjunct colleagues suffer is no better than a slacker professor who only wants to get by. From the perspective of a struggling adjunct, what their colleagues (slacker or otherwise) owe them is not more publications, student advising, or committee work for the university. Rather, what their colleagues owe them is empathy, validation, and tangible support. A slacker professor may be indifferent to their own academic accomplishment or advancement. They may not feel compelled to join yet another committee or task force. They may not take the initiative to direct another student thesis. But nothing suggests that a slacker professor is incapable of offering empathy, validation, or tangible support to their fellow adjunct colleagues. In short, the reality of deserving individuals struggling to find a job while slacker professors are doing the bare minimum is indeed unjust, but the answer to this injustice is not to have slacker professors do more work or to fire them to make room for the more deserving academics. Instead of assigning blame to the slacker professor, it is more pressing to address the structural issues that create the problem of deserving individuals not getting a job in the first place.

Let us now turn to the concern that slacker professors are objectionable because they perpetuate the stereotype of a lazy professor. The stereotype of a lazy professor, as I pointed out in Chapter 4, is just a stereotype. There are plenty of professors who continue to publish, mentor, and perform service diligently long after they receive tenure. Nevertheless, is the slacker professor doing their profession a disservice by perpetuating this stereotype? In recent years, conservatives have deployed this stereotype to attack the tenure system or to justify budget cuts to higher education. The stakes seem particularly high when the stereotype is tied to the future of higher education. So one can imagine the frustration of a professor seeking to correct the perception of a lazy academic, only to have their colleague confirm the very misconception they are trying to dispel.

In this case, I agree that the slacker professor is not being a very good sport. Nevertheless, "preserving the good name" of academics is not a sufficiently good reason to compel slacker professors to change their ways. In fact, I wonder if "preserving the good name" of a group is *ever* a sufficient reason to compel an individual member to change their way. Consider the stereotypical image of Asians "being too smart, too focused on academics, one-dimensional and lacking personal skills,"[5] as well as the stereotype of Asians being meek and quiet— both of which have contributed to the underrepresentation of Asians in leadership and executive positions in the United States.[6] Undoubtedly, there are Asians who fit these racial stereotypes. But should we then compel nerdy, socially awkward Asians to change their ways *because* they are perpetuating a harmful stereotype? Should we then hold quiet and submissive Asians responsible for the difficulties Asians face in the professional world? I think not. Instead of holding the *individual* responsible, we should address the ways such stereotypes have led to unfair treatment of Asians. It should not be the individual's burden to "correct" a stereotype; rather, we need to rethink what it takes to be a good leader or what it means to be socially competent. Similarly, in the case of the slacker academic, the burden is not on the individual slacker to conform to a more favorable image of an academic. Rather, we need to interrogate the assumptions that we make when we label an individual a slacker, as well as the dubious way the slacker academic stereotype is being deployed to justify budget cuts to higher education. In sum, the slacker academic should not be compelled to change their way *simply* because they may perpetuate a stereotype.

Finally, it is worth noting that what counts as "just enough" work varies from one institution to another, or even one generation to another. While this does not necessarily justify slacking, it does show that the idea of a slacker academic is slippery at best. One university's slacker may very well be another university's go-getter. Each institution has its own standard and culture of work. A professor in a demanding university may have to publish more articles or teach more courses than a professor in a less demanding institution. Academics of the older generation may not have needed any publications to get a job offer decades ago when academia still had a robust job market. It is now standard that newly minted PhDs should have at least one publication (often more) if they wish to get any job interviews. Our understanding of "the bare minimum" is not static—it varies and evolves with the culture and the individuals within it. The publish-or-perish culture in academia tends to favor go-getters. And the more go-getters we generate in academia, the more normalized the culture of hyper-productivity becomes.

Ironically, the go-getters may have even inadvertently "created" slackers (or the perception of slackers) by raising the standard of what is "good enough." The go-getters raise the standard or expectations in two ways. First, at a university where most faculty publish two to three articles for tenure, a professor who publishes five is certainly going above and beyond. As long as the prolific professor is the outlier, those who publish two to three articles are not considered slackers. But now imagine the university hires more and more go-getters; publishing five or more articles would likely become the new norm, and professors who publish only two to three articles may be perceived as slackers. Second, the go-getters may change expectations not just in terms of what counts as the "bare minimum" or "good enough," but also what counts as an acceptable work ethic. In an institution where most professors are content with just meeting the minimal requirement, doing just enough is enough. And if everyone is a slacker, then no one really is a slacker. But suppose the go-getters have now reached a critical mass, going above and beyond will then become the new standard. In other words, it is no longer good enough to be just good enough. Of course, the irony here is that when everyone is a go-getter, then going above and beyond becomes the new "good enough."

SLACKERS ARE SOURCES OF EMOTIONAL DISTRESS TO OTHERS

Suppose we have a slacker who does just enough to get by. They perform their assigned tasks, though they never do more than what is asked of them. Is slacking still objectionable if the slacker is not burdening anyone else? Who is the slacker really harming by being unambitious or underachieving? Consider, for example, a slacker student with a trust fund substantial enough to cover his tuition and life beyond college. Suppose this slacker student attends college mainly to placate his parents—he chooses an easy major, goes to just enough classes to keep his attendance, does his fair share of work when he does group projects, and studies just enough to get a C. But the bare minimum is the extent of effort the slacker is willing to make. He spends the rest of his time drinking and partying. This slacker student isn't interested in his education, nor is he concerned about having a career post-college due to his wealth. With his average intelligence and considerable financial resources, the slacker student could certainly do better. He can afford private tutors or supplemental textbooks, for example. But he simply can't bring himself to care.

Given his trust fund, it is not obvious what kind of tangible harm (if any) the slacker student is inflicting on others. He is not imposing a financial strain on his parents the way a student whose parents co-sign their student loan might be. Some may find his slacker attitude unsavory and self-centered, but that speaks to a character flaw, rather than a burden or harm to others. Others may find his slackerdom a waste of resources, but the same could be said of anyone who squanders their fortune, not just the slacker. But let us look beyond material harm, as harm need not be measured in economic terms exclusively.

One may argue that even if a slacker is not burdening others financially, their lack of direction can still be distressing to others, especially to those who are emotionally invested in their success. Even if there is no student loan to repay, even if the slacker student is not going to live in his parents' basement post-college, he can still cause emotional distress to those around him. The slacker's parents, for example, are likely to be disappointed by their slacker child's underachievement, if not distressed by his apathetic attitude. They may even blame themselves for failing at parenting. In other words, the slacker's underachievement can easily become a source of stress and frustration for those who care about his well-being. Nevertheless, being hurt is not the same as being wronged. Suppose I tell a friend how I feel about our friendship and their moral character. The truth may be harsh and hurtful—but that doesn't mean I have wronged my friend. So, the relevant question here is whether the emotional distress caused by the slacker is unjust. Has the slacker wronged his parents by not making the best of himself? Does being the source of disappointment and frustration make one blameworthy? Does the slacker child owe it to anyone, especially those who care about him, to actualize his potential?

Consider, for example, that a young artist with a precocious talent for painting is offered a prestigious fine art scholarship. Despite her considerable talent and potential, our young artist declines the scholarship in order to pursue her interest in gymnastics. Insofar as her pursuit in gymnastics is driven by enthusiasm rather than talent, it is all but certain that our wannabe gymnast is trading a promising career in art for a mediocre one in sports. Both accomplished artists, the parents had hoped that their child would continue the family tradition. They are disappointed in their child for giving up a remarkable opportunity. They are distressed by the possibility of their child squandering her exceptional talent in painting. But the most serious blow, for the parents, is the fact that their child seems to care very little about painting, despite having an unusual gift for it.

Like the slacker, our wannabe gymnast is also a source of disappointment and frustration for her parents. Like the slacker, our wannabe gymnast is likely to underachieve (in comparison with what she could have achieved with her career as an artist). So, should we blame our wannabe gymnast for failing to achieve her potential the way we blame our slacker? Perhaps some of us would find her decision imprudent; perhaps some of us would feel let down that our world is deprived of a talented artist. But it is inappropriate to say that she owes her parents—or any of us for that matter—to actualize her potential in fine art. Our wannabe gymnast has not *wronged* her parents by disappointing and distressing them. After all, parents everywhere are constantly disappointed and distressed by their children for all sorts of reasons. Some parents are disappointed when their children don't call home every day; some parents are distressed when their children go camping. It seems unreasonable to hold children accountable for disappointing or distressing their parents. Minimally, being a source of disappointment and frustration in and of itself is not a wrong—there have to be some additional factors that make being a source of disappointment or frustration wrong.

So is our wannabe gymnast any different from our slacker? One may argue that our wannabe gymnast is making an effort, whereas our slacker is not. One may argue that it is the willingness to make something of oneself that makes all the difference. Given that our wannabe gymnast is still committed to making something of herself in a different field, her underachievement can be justified. Her artist parents might be disappointed and frustrated, but they cannot fault her for not trying in life. The slacker, by contrast, is not making an effort (that goes beyond doing the bare minimum). It is the lack of effort that makes his underachievement indefensible, and the emotional burden he places on his parents inexcusable. Put differently: while it's true that both the wannabe gymnast and the slacker disappoint others, the underachievement of the former is justified, whereas the underachievement of the latter is not. Accordingly, we may excuse the wannabe gymnast for causing disappointment, but the same cannot be said about the slacker.

Admittedly, the reason for disappointment matters. Disappointing someone by failing to honor a promise is different from disappointing someone by failing to inflate their ego. Nevertheless, the issue is not settled by simply pointing out that the wannabe gymnast makes an effort, whereas the slacker doesn't. What we are trying to settle here is what makes *slacking* blameworthy. We want to know what is especially bad about an underachievement caused by slacking, as opposed to an underachievement caused by giving up a promising career in favor of a non-career-driven interest. We want to know what makes the slacker more blameworthy than the wannabe gymnast when they are both inflicting disappointment on their parents.

Recall that one of the defining features of a slacker is precisely their lack of effort. Slacking is, by definition, not making an effort (beyond the bare minimum). To say that the slacker is blameworthy *because* they don't make an effort is a tautology. It is simply rewording the definition and masquerading it as an explanation. It is akin to saying that a burglar is blameworthy because they burgle or that an assassin is blame-worthy because they kill. It is obviously true that a slacker doesn't make an effort, but that alone does not tell us why they are blameworthy. To avoid a tautological explanation, we need something other than "the lack of effort" to explain why slacking is bad.

THE FETISHIZATION OF "EFFORT"

Why do we excuse the wannabe gymnast for her undera-chievement simply because she's made an effort? There is something rather odd about our attachment to the effort, especially if we don't expect the effort to pay off. Let's look at the return of the slacker's and wannabe gymnast's respective investments. (By "investment," I mean the effort they make; and by "return," their achievement.) The slacker's return is at least proportionate to his lack of investment, whereas the wannabe gymnast's achievement (or lack thereof) is dispro-portionate to her invested effort. At the end of the day, she is just not that good of a gymnast. So, the gymnast is "wasting" her time and energy on a pursuit that yields minimal success. Contra the gymnast, the slacker may end up having a better return in investment by making the minimal effort. There is no disappointment because there is no expectation to begin with, and no "wasted" time or energy because the slacker expended none.

Granted, the wannabe gymnast is pursuing her passion, so she may find pleasure in the pursuit itself, even if it doesn't result in any noteworthy professional accomplishment. But we do often speak of "making an effort" as a duty, even if the effort involved seems futile or unpleasant to the agent. We do think of making an effort as having an intrinsic value. Imagine that a couple on the verge of divorce signs up for couples counseling even though they detest counseling and see little point to the endeavor. Still, they may want to "make an effort" so they can say in good faith that they have done everything they could to salvage the marriage. Or consider a patient with a terminal illness willing to undergo an agonizing experimental treatment, even though the odds are not in their favor. The patient themselves may not even want to undergo the treatment, but they still want to show their family that they are trying. Or consider the ongoing pro-democracy movement in Hong Kong, where protesters have taken to the streets to voice their dissent since June 2019. Since then, the mainland Chinese government has increasingly tightened its control of the semi-autonomous region. As a result, protesters readily acknowledge that their effort will most likely amount to nothing. Yet, many of them are unwilling to "go down without a fight."[7] While many see subjugation by the mainland Chinese government as inevitable, Hong Kong protesters consider it their duty to persevere.

When it comes to self-betterment, the stakes may not be as high as the stakes in mending a marriage, staying alive, or standing up against a totalitarian regime. These examples are meant to demonstrate ways in which we consider effort as something valuable in and of itself. Some of us may even consider making an effort a matter of duty. And this reflects our attitude toward work: the need to be productive is so ingrained in our culture that we give credit to those who at least *act* productively (i.e., making an effort), even if their action yields no profit in the end. We value effort because it demonstrates one's commitment to work, and this commitment stems from the primacy of *doing* in our culture. We detest the slacker not because they fail, but because they don't act in a way that is consistent with a productive citizen.

What is it about "effort" that we value so much? The Protestant work ethic at the heart of our productivity culture may once again offer some insights. In the Introduction, we saw that for the Calvinists, work does not grant us salvation, as we are justified before God by faith alone. We are saved not because we have somehow "merited" our place in heaven with our good deeds; rather, we are saved solely by God's grace. Importantly, even though work is not a means to salvation, it is still indicative of our faith in God. The harder we work, the deeper our faith. We do not know for certain whether we were elected by God, but we have to act *as* if we were saved. We have to behave and work *as* someone who is confident in their salvation. In other words, even if our salvation is uncertain, we still have to make an effort to prove to ourselves that we are the kind of individuals who could be saved. The fetishization of effort, then, may very well be a legacy of the Calvinist work ethic that continues to animate our productivity culture. For the Calvinists, work—even when salvation is never guaranteed—attests to our faith in God. For us, making an effort—even when the payoff is unclear—demonstrates our commitment to the ethos of productivity.

Effort matters. In Chapter 6, we will turn to Immanuel Kant, a philosopher who believes that it is *striving* for, rather than reaching, the perfection that counts. An effortless accomplishment, however impressive, does not actually demonstrate the rational nature that makes us uniquely human. Effort matters because it is only when we put in work that our accomplishment becomes meaningful. Once again, Kant will bring us back to the relationship between being and doing, who we are and what we do.

What If Everyone Were a Slacker?

6

In this chapter, I will look at a different version of the freeloading problem, using Enlightenment philosopher Immanuel Kant (1724–1804), as my resource. As we will see, Kant argues that we have a duty to self-cultivate given the kind of creatures that we are. This means we ought not to be satisfied with doing "just enough" to get by. We must go above and beyond our basic capacities. We must develop skills that enable us to pursue goals that are proper to who we are (i.e., rational beings). Even though much of this chapter is on Kant, my purpose here is not exegetical. My reason for engaging Kant in this chapter is twofold: first, I believe he makes a compelling case against slacking that helps explain our aversion to freeloaders, even if such freeloaders do not impose an undue burden on others. Second, in Chapter 1, we saw various philosophical attempts to promote leisure as the more autonomous or dignified way of living. The idea that anti-industriousness offers a form of existential freedom is a reaction to—and an inversion of—the Enlightenment ideal that links productivity to subjectivity. As we will see in this chapter, Kant's argument explicitly links *being* and *doing*, who we are and what we do. Engaging with his argument will hopefully give us a better understanding of why, in a debate on slacking, our very conception of self is at stake.

Recall in Chapter 5, I focused primarily on whether free-loaders or "parasitic slackers" have wronged others by imposing an undue burden on them. I argued that: 1) slackers need not be freeloaders, for freeloading is an incidental, rather than essential, quality of slacking; (2) even if a slacker were freeloading, it doesn't necessarily involve burdening others (as in the case of the slacker student with a substantial trust fund); and (3) even when a freeloader does impose an undue burden, what we object to is the sense of entitlement, rather than the slacking in and of itself.

With this in mind, let's examine the question "What if everyone were a slacker?" The assumption behind this question, as I take it, is that a world in which no one cares to make something of themselves is undesirable. After all, most things that we enjoy in our life are a product of someone else's labor or talent. The richness of our life is very much dependent on the ingenuity and labor of others. As such, a world in which everyone is a slacker—a world in which everyone is doing the bare minimum to get by—is not a world that we, including the slackers, desire. Here's why.

Suppose you are a slacker and you don't care to make something of yourself. It doesn't mean that you are absolutely devoid of skills. You still have to survive after all. It does, however, mean that you are content with developing just the skills that are necessary for your survival, and you never bother to go above and beyond. You learned how to ride a bicycle so you can get to work, you learned how to cook instant noodles so you don't starve to death, and you work just enough hours to make your rent and buy your instant noodles. But even a slacker such as yourself would still prefer a world full of richness, as opposed to a world that is dull and austere. Even a slacker such as yourself would still want to enjoy the pleasure that goes beyond basic survival. Suppose you spend all day watching Netflix, someone would have to make the TV shows that you binge-watch; suppose you love getting high, someone would have to grow the weed that you so enjoy smoking. In other words, the kind of world a slacker prefers is the kind in which *other people* go above and beyond their basic capacities to cultivate world-enriching talents. But if this were the case, isn't it rather hypocritical of you to insist on being a slacker, and yet wish others to be useful? What makes *you* so special that you get to enjoy the fruits of others' labor without making any contribution?

Here, we have a different version of the freeloading problem. Specifically, we object to the slacker on the grounds that they fail to make a positive contribution to the world. It is not enough that the slacker doesn't impose an undue burden on others—they also have to make a positive contribution to the richness of the world. Put differently, it is not enough that you don't harm; you also have to help. This particular rendition of the freeloader problem can be traced all the way back to the work of Kant. The "what if everyone does X" question bears resemblance to his Formula of the Universal Law of Nature, to which we will now turn.

In *Groundwork for the Metaphysics of Morals*, Kant presents the Formula of the Universal Law of Nature as follows, "Act only in accordance with that maxim through which you can at the same time will that it become a universal law."[1] Consider "maxim" as a plan of action; for example, I will feed my neighbor's cat if she is out of town. The Formula is supposed to help us adjudicate the permissibility of our plan of action. The basic idea is the following: before you act, ask yourself whether you can "universalize" your maxim. What would it be like if everyone (i.e., every rational being) adopts your maxim? What would it be like if everyone in your circumstance were to act the way you plan on acting? First, we have to determine whether such a world is even conceivable. If universalizing your plan of action would undermine the feasibility of the very action that you seek to perform, then a world in which everyone acts like you do is not in fact conceivable.

One example by Kant involves a man making a false promise in order to get out of a sticky situation. For a false promise to work, the man needs *someone* to believe in him. However, if everyone can just make a false promise whenever it suits them, then the very idea of promise-making would become a joke, as no one would believe in anyone anymore. And "no one would believe in anyone anymore" is a direct contradiction to what the man is trying to achieve—to get someone to believe in his false promise. In other words, as soon as he universalizes his maxim, he undermines the feasibility of his own lie. Therefore, the original principle of action (I'll make a false promise) is actually inconsistent with the world in which that principle is universalized (a world that lacks promising altogether). As such, a world in which everyone adopts his maxim is in fact inconceivable; this, in turn, tells us that the act of making a false promise is impermissible.

How might we apply the Formula of Universal Law of Nature to slacking, then? Luckily for us, one of Kant's examples takes up the question of self-development. Kant writes:

> A third [man] finds in himself a talent, which could, by means of some cultivation, make him into a human being who is useful for all sorts of aims. But he sees himself as in comfortable circumstances and sooner prefers to indulge in gratification than to trouble himself with the expansion and improvement of his fortunate natural

predispositions. Yet he still asks whether, apart from the agreement of his maxim of neglecting his gifts of nature with his propensity to amusement, it also agrees with what one calls "duty." Then he sees that, although a nature could still subsist in accordance with such a universal law, though then the human being (like the South Sea Islanders) would think only of letting his talents rust and applying his life merely to idleness, amusement, procreation, in a word, to enjoyment; yet it is impossible for him to will that this should become a universal law of nature, or that it should be implanted in us as such by natural instinct. For as a rational being he necessarily wills that all the faculties in him should be developed, because they are serviceable and given to him for all kinds of possible aims.[2]

Here, Kant once again asks us to employ the same procedure with the Formula of the Universal Law of Nature. You are a slacker who is nevertheless rational enough to ask yourself, "What if everyone slacks? What if no one cares to develop any talents or skills?" Unlike the maxim of making a false promise, a world in which no one develops their talent is at least *conceivable*. There is nothing contradictory or self-undermining about universalizing slacking. We would just have a boring world full of idlers. Yet, according to Kant, that's not the end of the story. For we still have to ask, "Is this a world I would rationally want to live in?"

In the passage quoted above, Kant maintains that as a rational being, the individual "necessarily wills that all the faculties in him should be developed, because they are serviceable and given to him for all kinds of possible aims."[3] But why is it the case? The operative term here is "rational being."

For Kant, it is because of our unique nature as a rational being that we "necessarily will" to cultivate our talents. To see why this is the case, let us turn to a different passage. In *Metaphysics of Morals*, Kant writes:

> Man has a duty to himself to cultivate (*cultura*) his natural powers (powers of spirit, mind, and body), as means to all sorts of possible ends. Man owes it to himself (as a rational being) not to leave idle and, as it were, rusting away the natural predispositions and capacities that his reason can someday use [...] for, as a being capable of ends (of making objects his ends), he must owe the use of his powers not merely to natural instinct but rather to the freedom by which he determines their scope. Hence the basis on which man should develop his capacities (for all sorts of ends) is not regard for the advantages that their cultivation can provide [...] Instead, it is a command of morally practical reason and a duty of man to himself to cultivate his capacities (some among them more than others, insofar as men have different ends), and to be in a pragmatic respect a man equal to the end of his existence.[4]

For Kant, the reason we ought to cultivate our capacities is not that it is beneficial to us. Developing one's talents is a moral, rather than a practical (or prudential), matter.[5] Of course, failing to develop one's capacities makes it rather difficult to live one's life, even if one never reflects on or revises one's own goals. So it would be prudent for one to develop at least some talents. (Recall, a slacker is not devoid of skills. They do need some skills to survive.) But for Kant, the duty to develop our talents has everything to do with the kind of creatures that we are. In other words, there is a link between *being* and *doing*, who we are and what we do.

In the Introduction, we saw that for Aristotle, human flourishing is achievable only when we live a life in which we actualize our characteristic function: rationality. Rationality is the function that makes us who we are as humans. So, in order to be virtuous, to live a flourishing life proper to who we are, we must exercise our rationality. Like Aristotle (and many other philosophers), Kant believes that the capacity to reason is what distinguishes humans from other animals.[6] As rational beings, we are capable of setting ends (goals) for ourselves, as opposed to being governed by our instincts. More importantly, being an end-setter means that we have the freedom that non-rational creatures lack. With the aid of rationality, we get to select life goals that go beyond survival. Our life purpose need not be confined to satisfying our natural needs. To accomplish our self-selected goals, we need to develop *at least some* of our talents, talents that go beyond our basic survival needs. Suppose I have set my goal to become a standup comedian. In order to achieve this goal, I must cultivate relevant capacities, such as public speaking and comedy writing. Importantly, I have a duty to develop my talents not because it serves instrumental purposes such as having a good career, making my parents proud, or being able to pay my rent. My effort to develop my capacities is instrumental (or morally pragmatic) only in the sense that it allows me to *be* the kind of person that is proper to whom I am meant to be. That is, to be a rational creature who has the freedom to set their own goal.

Consider the language of "cultivation" in the quoted passage above. For Kant, the perfection of our talents must be obtained through "*deeds*, not in mere *gifts* [...] indebted to nature."[7] The kind of talents that are proper to our status as rational goal-setters is the kind that involves effort and work; it is not simply a natural gift bestowed on us by the luck of the draw. For Kant, it makes little sense to speak of the cultivation of one's talent as a duty, if it is something that is simply handed to us. If we were already at the peak of our talent, we would not feel the weight of this duty to develop ourselves. A genius composer who can write a piece of musical score effortlessly would not have a "duty" to perfect themselves, for example. Yet, since most of us are not geniuses, self-improvement presents itself as a duty (what we owe to ourselves). Accordingly, the emphasis is on the perfecting, rather than the perfection. Or, as Kant puts it, it is our "duty to strive for this perfection, but not to reach it" (emphases in original).[8]

We have taken a detour to make sense of Kant's claim that "as a rational being," one "necessarily wills that all the faculties in him should be developed."[9] In this Kantian account, our worthiness is determined by whether we live a life that is proper to us as rational beings. As goal-setters, rational beings can deliberate and choose the kind of life they desire. This doesn't mean that rational beings always get to live the way they want, unhindered by circumstances. However, it does mean that rational beings can set their own goals and take steps to achieve them (and that typically involves developing at least some skills). So, given the kind of creature we are, we "necessarily" will that we develop our faculties in order to pursue the goals we set for ourselves. This includes both present goals that we have set, as well as future goals that we may set for ourselves (although it is more likely that we would focus on developing faculties that would help us with our present goals).

With Kant in mind, let's return to the slacker and the wannabe gymnast that we encountered in Chapter 5. Both of them are underachieving. Both of them are a disappointment in the eyes of their parents. And yet somehow the slacker is deemed more blameworthy than the wannabe gymnast (if she were to be blamed at all). One explanation we considered briefly is that effort matters. The wannabe gymnast's underachievement is justified because at least she tries to make something of herself, whereas the slacker's underachievement is unjustified because he is not making any effort at all. Recall in Chapter 5, I argued that we need something other than "the lack of effort" to explain why slacking is bad in order to avoid a tautological explanation. It seems that Kant has offered one here. To borrow his language, the wannabe gymnast's effort shows that she is living a life that is proper to what it means to be a human: to be a goal-setter. A slacker, however, is not living up to what he is meant to be—not just in terms of his wasted talent, but also the failure to *choose* a goal in life. He is willing to take his "purpose" (fulfillment of natural needs) as something given to him. He is a passive recipient of his own goals and takes no responsibility for them.

With this explanation, we at least have an account of the slacker's blameworthiness that is not tautological. As rational beings, we have the freedom to live in a way that is not wholly determined by our instincts or environment. Our life purpose is something that we can choose and own, not just given (by nature or others). While a slacker may very well develop basic skills for survival, the slacker does not care to cultivate skills that go above and beyond their basic necessities or environment. They learned how to ride a bicycle because they needed to get to their job; they learned how to make instant noodles because that's the easiest way to prevent starvation. The slacker fails to make something of themselves insofar as they fail to be a goal-setter. The kind of skills the slacker acquires is not commensurable with the kind of goals that a rational being *could have* set for themselves. As such, the slacker is at fault for leading the kind of life that makes them indistinguishable from a mere animal, unworthy of who they are meant to be. Or, using Kant's words, the slacker has failed to be someone who is "equal to the end of [their] existence."[10]

* * *

Let us return to an earlier scenario, where our rational slacker deploys the Formula of the Universal Law of Nature and asks, "What if everyone were a slacker?" Even though the rational slacker can conceive of a world in which everyone slacks, such a world is not the kind of world that the slacker would rationally want to live in (given that they would still prefer an enriching rather than an improvised world for their own indulgences). What exactly is the slacker's fault, then? For one thing, we are bothered by the slacker's hypocrisy. For another, we are bothered by their sense of entitlement, that they feel comfortable to partake in the fruits of other's labor without offering anything in return. With this in mind, let us now return to Kant's *Groundwork* one more time.

After considering the Formula of the Universal Law of Nature, Kant goes on to discuss the Formula of Humanity, which goes as follows, "Act so that you use humanity, as much in your own person as in the person of every other, always at the same time as end and never merely as means."[11] Simply put, the Formula of Humanity forbids us to treat any rational being, including one's own self, as a mere instrument. (For Kant, we also owe a duty to ourselves, and it is possible for us to use ourselves as a mere instrument.[12]) Rational beings are not "things" that exist solely for instrumental purposes; rather, they command our respect by virtue of their rationality.

So, the Formula demands us to respect each person, insofar as they are rational, as their own end. This explains why making a false promise fails the Formula of Humanity. By deceiving others, one is treating another rational being simply as a means to one's end. Suppose you ask your friend to give you a ride home, promising that you'd be the designated driver when you all go out next week. You know full well that you won't be able to drive because your license has been suspended. This is you treating your friend as a mere means (a chauffeur) to your own end (to get home).

What about slacking then? Is a slacker using others as a means only? Perhaps an argument could be made that a slacker who imposes an undue burden on others is using others as a means only (say, a 30-year-old man who refuses to get a job and leeches off his parents). But what about a slacker who doesn't impose an undue burden on others, a slacker who simply doesn't care to make something of himself? The charge of "using others as a means only" does not seem to apply to these "self-sufficient" slackers. Yet we must not forget that the slacker is also a rational being. So, the trickier question here is whether the slacker is using *himself* as a means only by failing to develop his talent.

One way to think about this is that a slacker fails to take responsibility for setting any goal that goes beyond what is already "assigned" to them by nature (e.g., getting food, procreating), so the slacker is subordinating their rational nature to a merely natural goal. In this sense, the slacker may be said to be using himself as a means only. Granted, this is not a particularly intuitive way to think about the wrongness of slacking (that the slacker is using himself as a mere means). But something else Kant says may help here. For Kant, there is more to the Formula of Humanity than the prohibition of instrumentalizing rational beings. Regarding one's duty to develop talent, Kant writes:

> [It] is not enough that the action does not conflict with humanity in our person as end in itself; it must also *harmonize with it*. Now in humanity there are predispositions to greater perfection, which belong to ends of nature in regard to the humanity in our subject; to neglect these would at most be able to subsist with the *preservation* of humanity as end in itself, but not with the *furthering* of this end (emphases in original).[13]

In other words, it is not enough that we refrain from treating a person as a mere means; we must also "harmonize with" and "further" humanity. Even if a slacker were not using anyone as a means only, they still fail to "further" humanity. That is, even if the slacker were not imposing an undue burden on others, they are still at fault for failing to offer anything in return when they clearly have the ability to do so.

* * *

At this point, a defense of slackers is not looking too promising. For one thing, the slacker is living a life unworthy of who they are. They could have done a lot more with themselves, yet they choose to develop only the most basic skills to get by. For another, the slacker is hypocritical and selfish. They can see that a world in which everyone is a slacker is not a world they desire, and yet they continue to freeload on the hard work and talents of others. If we follow Kant's Formula of Universal Law of Nature, it is especially evident that a slacker is being hypocritical and selfish. After all, they are acting on a maxim (not developing talents) that they know is not universalizable. And by doing so, the slacker is essentially making an exception for themselves. They are singling out themselves as *special*— someone who is allowed to act in a way that other people are not allowed to act. Now, is it possible to defend such a selfish, unworthy individual (or, as Aaron James would say, an "asshole"[14])?

Let's begin with the charge of selfishness. Someone who is always the taker and never the giver is indeed selfish. I don't have a defense of selfishness. However, a slacker need not be selfish as an individual *in general*. Many of us have this stereotypical image of a slacker as an indifferent teenager who cares only about themselves. Yet, nothing in my definition of slackers suggests that they have to be uncaring toward others. In fact, it is quite conceivable that someone who doesn't care about self-development is still a generous individual in other respects. A slacker stoner may have done nothing productive all day, but if their elderly neighbor asked for help, they would gladly offer their service. A slacker student may have signed up for the easiest major and studied just enough to get an adequate GPA, but when their roommate lost their job and couldn't pay the rent, the slacker did not hesitate to cover their share for the month. A slacker academic may not be interested in furthering their own research and career, and they may be considered a freeloader when it comes to the production of knowledge. But this same slacker academic can still be a caring mentor or a generous colleague. What a slacker does not care about is their *personal* development or accomplishment, but that need not preclude them from having concerns for the well-being of others. In other words, the slacker may be "selfish" to the extent that they freeload on other people's skills and talents, but the slacker is not necessarily selfish in all aspects of their life. There may very well be altruistic or generous individuals who simply don't care to make something of themselves.

If this were the case, chastising slackers on the grounds of their selfishness becomes less compelling. At most, we can say that a slacker is selfish *to the extent* that they single themselves out as an exception when it comes to the duty to develop oneself. So a slacker may be called selfish in this narrow and specific sense, but they need not be selfish in a general sense. After all, do we really want to call someone selfish when they care more about other people's welfare than their personal development? Is the slacker student who helps out their roommate "selfish" simply because they don't put in the work in their philosophy assignment? It seems that we would have to really stretch the meaning of selfishness to make the charge stick. Now, there are certainly slackers who are selfish through and through, and not simply in a narrow sense of exempting themselves from self-betterment. But there are also go-getters who are selfish through and through, it just so happens that they care about self-betterment. In other words, like entitlement, selfishness (in a general sense) may just be an incidental, rather than an essential, quality of a slacker.

Let's now turn to the charge of hypocrisy. Suppose we agree that a slacker is only selfish in the narrow sense and that a slacker can be a generous person overall. Still, it seems rather hypocritical for the slacker to want other people to do what they are unwilling to do. As we saw earlier, even though slackers are unwilling to make something of themselves, they nevertheless prefer a world in which *other people* make something of themselves. So, even if they are not selfish, the slacker may still be hypocritical.

I agree that being hypocritical is not an appealing quality in general. But does the slackers' "hypocrisy" necessarily commit them to change their way? Consider the following. Suppose a woman adores children. She believes that children bring delight to the world and that a world in which people procreate is preferable. And let's say this woman has all the necessary qualities to be a good parent: patience, a sense of responsibility, affection for children, and so on. She has an excellent support system; she is also financially secured enough that raising a child would not present an undue financial burden. And yet, she does not want to have a child because she also values having flexibility in her schedule and private time when she comes home from work. She would just rather dote on someone else's children. In other words, she loves children, and she would not want to live in a world without children; and yet, she is unwilling to raise a child herself. Would we want to say that this woman is being selfish or hypocritical for preferring a world in which *other people* make the effort to parent, even though she is unwilling to commit to parenthood herself? Would we really want to say to this woman, "You ought to become a parent. You ought to procreate because the kind of world in which no one is willing to parent is not a world you desire"?—I think not.

But if we are unwilling to condemn or pressure a child-loving woman to have children, then why would we tell the slacker (who prefers a world with non-slackers) that they ought to make something of themselves? In fact, there are certain qualities that might not even make sense to universalize. Suppose we value good leadership qualities, and we would not want to live in a world in which no one cares to be a leader. What follows from this? Does it mean we want *everyone* to cultivate leadership skills? A world in which everyone cultivates their leadership skill is not necessarily desirable. Who else is left to be led if everyone wants to practice their leadership skills? It doesn't seem unreasonable for someone to say, "I don't want to be a leader, I am not interested in cultivating any leadership skills. But I hope *other people* would strive to be a leader. I want someone else to cultivate leadership skills because I believe a society with effective, compassionate leaders is preferable." Might the slacker offer a similar line of reasoning? Might the slacker say, "I don't want to be useful; I am not interested in cultivating any skill beyond what is necessary. But I hope other people strive to be useful. I want someone else to cultivate their talents because I believe a society with talented individuals is preferable"?

One last point about universalizing slacking. Suppose we agree that no one wants to live in a world in which everyone is a slacker—not even the slacker themselves. From this supposed truism, the anti-slackers infer, "No one (rationally) endorses slackerdom." I have been staging my defense by responding to this claim. However, I believe there is an alternate explanation for our objection to a world full of slackers. Our aversion to a world full of slackers may have nothing to do with slackers. Our aversion may simply be an aversion to a homogeneous world in which everyone comes from the same mold. One may not want a world full of slackers simply because one values diversity—one doesn't want a world full of any one kind of individuals. The same individual may also hold the view that a world full of go-getters is not a world they would want to live in. Put differently, even if it is true that no one wants to live in a world full of slackers, the issue may have more to do with the lack of diversity or extreme conformity, rather than slacking in and of itself.

Finally, let us examine the complaint that slackers are not living a life proper to who they are. What can we say to defend the slacker's "unworthiness"? In *Idleness*, Brian O'Conner challenges the Kantian imperative that we ought to make ourselves worthy of who we are. He wonders what it would take to motivate the idler (in our case, the slacker) to change their way of living. He finds it incredulous that the idler would all of a sudden become interested in placing their lifestyle under the scrutiny of the Universal Law of Nature. Why would an idler bother to ask, "What if everyone were an idler?" They weren't interested in this question before, why now? As long as idleness is working for them, the idler seems to have little motivation to question the way they live. Kant is thus assuming two things here, according to O'Conner. First, Kant assumes that "his idler is amenable to the kinds of reasons for action [he] favors."[15] That is, Kant assumes that the idler cares about the universalizability of their maxims. And second, that "the idler finds something interesting in the question of what kind of person he would make of himself."[16] That is, Kant assumes that the idler worries about whether their idleness would make their life less worthy.

O'Conner offers an interesting strategy here. Instead of defending the worthiness of the idler, O'Conner questions the *relevance* of worthiness. Instead of arguing that idlers are in fact useful or worthy in some unexpected ways, O'Conner reminds us that the idler may not even be playing our game. The idler lives the way they do not because they embrace some alternate vision of worthiness (like the principled slackers in Richard Linklater's *Slacker*). Rather, worthiness may just be the kind of concern about which the idler has never given a thought. Admonishing the idler that the way they live is unworthy is akin to warning a vegan that there is a shortage of pork in the supermarkets or telling a young child that if they don't get out of bed now they would miss the weather report on the news. The idler, the vegan, and the child would simply respond, "who cares?" So O'Conner's strategy here is not that we need to prove an idler's worthiness, but rather to challenge the importance of worthiness. The charge of unworthiness is meaningful to the idler only if they care about being worthy in the first place. The idler delivers the most forceful rejection of our productivity culture (albeit inadvertently). They reject it not by protesting it—they reject it by *not thinking* about it.[17]

As we saw in Chapter 1, O'Conner is interested in exposing and challenging the "worthiness myth," a legacy of the Enlightenment. It is a myth that tells the "uplifting story about how we human beings can overcome those human tendencies we take to be based in nature: the greater the effort, the more impressive and worthy the result."[18] So, what happens when someone doesn't subscribe to the "worthiness myth"? Let us return to the slacker student that we encountered earlier. Suppose we now tell the slacker student, "You ought to live a life worthy of who you are; you ought not degrade yourself to a mere animal." This demand has any teeth to it only if our slacker student already accepts that being worthy is a goal worth pursuing, or that our worthiness is contingent upon our rejection of our animality, or even that there is something wrong or degrading about living like an animal. Absent these presumptions, it is not clear why the slacker student should feel *compelled* by this demand to be worthy. In fact, isn't this demand just another way to say that we ought to live up to our potential? Instead of "you ought to develop your academic potential. You ought not waste your talent," we now tell the slacker student, "you ought to exercise your freedom and rationality, you ought not waste the faculty bestowed upon you as a rational being." But why would the slacker student be any more motivated by the new imperative than the old one? Why would the slacker student feel compelled to live up to the potential of a rational being if they are not even compelled to live up to the potential of a student? What a slacker calls into question is precisely our compulsion to strive for the best.

Admittedly, the fact that a slacker is uninterested in living a worthy life does not necessarily justify the way they live. After all, a sociopathic serial killer may also be unconcerned with the feelings of their victims, but that wouldn't justify their sociopathic actions. But I think what O'Conner reminds us here is that the supposed truisms of "we ought to be the best version of ourselves" and "we ought to live a worthy life" may not be as self-evident as we take them to be. Of course, the anti-slackers or go-getters may protest, "How could anyone not care about being useful? How could anyone not care about being worthy?" But for the slacker, the value of self-development is precisely what they don't take for granted, and the relevance of worthiness is precisely what needs to be settled. What if "being good enough" (rather than "maximizing productivity") is our default attitude? What if we live in a world that doesn't put a premium on what one can produce? Instead of putting the slacker in the position of a defendant, perhaps it is we who ought to scrutinize the compulsion to "be the best version of oneself." Instead of challenging the slacker to defend themselves, perhaps the burden of proof is on the go-getter to give a defense of their go-getter ways. Would the go-getters be able to defend their way of life without appealing to some slippery notion of worthiness? Would they be able to conceive of a world in which being worthy or being useful is not an ideal that one strives for? I do not have answers to these questions. But luckily for me, my task is to defend the slacker, not the go-getter, and I shall not go above and beyond what I am tasked to do.

Imagine yourself at a party. The host, your friend, introduces you to another guest: "Get to know each other—I think you two will hit it off!" What would you say about yourself? And what sorts of questions might you ask your new acquaintance? Perhaps you'd start with generic, low-stake questions: "Where are you from?" "Have you seen [insert popular TV show]?" "Where did you get *that* jacket?"— and most likely of all, "What do you do?" Asking people what they do is not just an attempt to break the ice; it is also an effort to get to know a person. When we ask someone "what do you do?" we are also asking, "what kind of person are you?"

The social convention of getting to know someone through the kind of work they do brings us back to the connection between being and doing, between who we are and what we do. As we saw in Chapter 6, Kant offers an anti-slacking argument grounded in our rational nature. Our unique capacity to reason generates a special responsibility for us to cultivate our talents—to make ourselves useful. Accordingly, a failure to make something of ourselves is tantamount to a failure to *be* who we are. Kantian or not, many of us do self-identify through our work or accomplishments. We like to present ourselves by foregrounding what we take pride in, and we take pride in what we *do*. One may identify oneself as a data analyst, the guy who makes the best chai in town, a clinical ethicist with a PhD, or an essential worker during a pandemic. And if the slacker doesn't care to do anything, who are they really? If who we are is what we do, then what happens when the "doing" is taken out of the equation? So, one concern with regard to slacking is that the slacker is putting their very individuality at risk. Would the slacker still have a unique sense of self if they don't do anything?

Let's return to the party. What would it be like to have a "get-to-know-each-other" conversation with a slacker? What is there to "get to know" if the person does nothing all day? To be fair, a slacker doesn't just sit at home and stare at the wall all day. As we saw in Chapter 6, a slacker is not necessarily devoid of skills. After all, a slacker must acquire enough basic skills to survive—it's just that they don't cultivate any skills beyond those needed to serve their immediate, practical necessities. In the same vein, a slacker is not literally "doing nothing" all day. So, when asked, "what do you do?" the laziest slacker can still enumerate a variety of activities: getting out of bed, making coffee, shopping for groceries, playing video games, scrolling through Instagram feeds, walking from the couch to the fridge to get snacks, and so on. In fact, even "the Dude" from *The Big Lebowski* has to buy his own groceries and make his own White Russian; even the most stereotypical Hollywood pothead slacker still has to get out of bed to roll their joints. Furthermore, the average slacker is not as extreme as these slackers (the laziest slacker.) Most of the slackers we encounter every day probably have a job to which they devote minimal effort, such as Peter from *Office Space* and Dante from *Clerks*. If someone says to our average slacker "tell us what you do," they may very well offer a typical and conventionally respectable answer: "I have an office job," or, "I am a clerk at a convenience store." In other words, both the extreme slacker and the everyday slacker would have *something* to say if some-one were to ask them what they do.

Yet, if the point of asking "what do you do?" is to get to know someone, the slackers' answers don't seem to help at all. The extreme slacker may be able to give a list of mundane tasks that they perform throughout the day, but most of them are far too generic to tell us anything meaningful about the slacker *as an individual*. After all, most people also have to get up in the morning, make coffee, shop for groceries; many also play video games or scroll through their social media feeds during their spare time. For most of us, the hustle-and-bustle of everyday life is not really part of "who we are" in any meaningful sense. So, while it is true that the extreme slacker does "do things," the things they do seem to have little existential relevance.

What about the average, everyday slackers? Many of them do have a job. In fact, it is often in a work setting that we encounter such slackers. However, as long as the slacker's motto is to do the bare minimum to get by, they care lit-tle about what they do. They may very well be a responsible slacker who completes all their assigned tasks, but they don't care enough to do more than that. The slacker treats work simply as a matter of necessity. It is just a part of the routine of life, much like having to take out the trash at night or go to the laundromat on weekends. (Few—if any—would self-identify as "the guy who takes out the trash at night," or "the dude who does the laundry on weekends.") A job is probably as meaningless and forgettable for a slacker as our everyday routine is for us. Accordingly, knowing a slacker's day job is about as informative as knowing the sort of everyday routine that we do, and it wouldn't offer insight into who they are. In short, lacking any genuine investment in what they do, whatever occupation the slacker happens to have is unlikely to have a meaningful influence on how they perceive themselves as an individual.[1]

The point of this mental exercise—imagining what it is like to get to know a new acquaintance at a party—is to show our culturally ingrained conviction that one's work is the window into one's being. Accordingly, the slacker's lack of investment in their work raises the concern that their selfhood is at risk. How do we get to know a slacker? What is there to know? Do they even have a sense of who they are? However, before we try to "rescue" the slacker's individuality or identity, we need to interrogate the very connections between being and doing, who we are and what we do.

In a 1929 article titled "To 'Be' or to 'Do,'" James Truslow Adams (the writer who coined the term "American dream") laments that in the United States, "what a man *does* counts for so much more than what he *is*."[2] We care more about our career than our character. He chastises American universities for prioritizing doing over being—they are far more interested in training students to *do* things than to *be* someone. For Adams, vocational training such as medicine and engineering is not the same as a liberal arts education, for "one should teach us how to make a living, and the other how to live."[3] (Adams' remarks foreshadow Pieper's comments on the liberal arts and the servile arts. As we saw in Chapter 1, Pieper argues that with a liberal arts education, we are "liberated" from the mundane concerns for the practical, such as making rent or fixing a flat tire. We don't pursue knowledge in order to advance our career, rather we pursue it to enrich our mind.)

Adams is concerned that the overemphasis on doing may get in the way of being: "we are so busy *doing* that we have no time to *be*."[4] He worries that we may have lost sight of the fact that doing is merely an instrument to being, and that we have taken the means to be the end. He asks, "Is there any sense in doing if we are never to become something, to be something, as a result?"[5] In light of Adams' worry, it is all the more ironic that we now believe that who we are is what we do. Not only have we failed to subordinate doing to being, as Adams urges in his paper, but we have also actually come to *equate* doing with being. Our productivity culture has us believe that without doing, we cannot even be. The publish-or-perish ethos in academia powerfully captures the idea that without doing, we academics may as well cease to be.

With Adams' critique in mind, let's examine further our impulse to get to know someone through their profession. The default icebreaker "What do you do?" is not without its own perils, even if it may seem innocuous and low stakes at first glance. First, different jobs come with different stereotypes or expectations, and some jobs are considered more "respectable" than others. Since one is often judged or typecast by one's job, one's response to the simple icebreaker question is hardly value neutral or low stakes. If your new acquaintance works in a highly stigmatized profession, having to disclose what they do can be a source of embarrassment or even humiliation. Second, the stereotypes and expectations we assign to different jobs may very well impede our efforts to get to know someone. For example, if our new acquaintance is in a line of work that our society deems "respectable," we may inadvertently confer excessive credibility to them. Conversely, if our new acquaintance has a job that many deem unbecoming, we may develop biases against them before we get to know them. Certainly, there are times when it is appropriate or prudent to judge someone based on what they do for a living. Suppose your new acquaintance runs a human trafficking ring and their day-to-day job is to smuggle underage girls to work at underground brothels. It would not be unfair for you to judge them on the basis of what they do for a living. It doesn't matter what extenuating circumstances pushed them into this line of work; what they *do* is morally repugnant. Or suppose your new acquaintance is a healthcare worker who travels across the country to work at a COVID19-ravaged hotspot. It would not be unreasonable for you to immediately confer respect on your new acquaintance. But even so, given that many jobs are burdened with unwarranted assumptions and stigmas, perhaps we should check our impulse to deploy the "what do you do?" icebreaker when we try to get to know someone. This is not to say we should never inquire about the profession of a new acquaintance, but we ought to consider and explore alternative ways to get to know someone. In other words, we need to chip away at our ingrained assumption that what one does (for a living) tells us who one is.

The point I have made above is a derivative of a fairly obvious and uncontroversial idea—we should not prejudge a person based on what they do for a living. Nevertheless, one may worry that I have underestimated the existential importance of work by equating work with one's occupation. For what we do is more than just the job that pays the rent. When Kant speaks about our duty to develop our talents, he is not just talking about talents that we exclusively develop for our job. Rather, he is speaking more broadly about the kind of talents that would help us realize the goals we set for ourselves. So, one may argue that the "work" that tells us who we are may have nothing to do with our occupation, and thus what we do outside of our job may still have existential importance as long as we identify with this work. In other words, the link between doing and being is still legitimate as long as we don't exclusively restrict the meaning of "doing" to one's job.

Undoubtedly, we need to do more than swap business cards if we really want to get to know someone. For not everybody identifies with their job, and we can often get a better glimpse of who someone is by learning about their projects, hobbies, or community engagements. In fact, many of us identify ourselves with work that we find meaningful, and not necessarily with the work that pays our bills. For example, someone may say, "I wait tables at a restaurant for now, but I try to go to as many auditions as possible." We get a sense that this individual identifies more as an actor than a waiter, even if they have yet to land a role. They associate themselves with the career they hope to have, rather than the job that they do have. Or suppose someone says, "I manage a hedge fund, but more importantly I play drums in a band over the weekends." This hedge fund manager identifies more with their music than their day job. That is, their identity has more to do with their amateur interests than what they do for a living professionally. Accordingly, while we may not know or judge someone based on their job title, perhaps we can still know or judge them by what they do (or don't do!) outside of their job.

Suppose we agree that one's job title does not define who one is, as long as one does other things that are meaningful to one's identity. What does this mean for the slacker? If an everyday slacker is someone who doesn't try to make something of themselves, then it is unlikely that they would have much to show for outside of the job that they have (assuming that they have one). After all, taking the initiative to do projects, acquire hobbies, or engage in community service typically requires some effort beyond the bare minimum. However, it is also false that a slacker does absolutely nothing outside of work. A slacker may hang out with friends, watch a film, or play an occasional basketball game. But whatever extracurricular activities they do, they do them mostly to kill time or because that's what their friends or family want to do. They are not trying to become a film buff or a professional basketball player, nor are they motivated by a sense of purposefulness. And if the slacker happens to make themselves useful or if they happen to feel good about what they do, it's entirely unintentional and fortuitous. In short, even if a slacker has a life outside of work, their indifference toward their personal development means that they are unlikely to identify themselves with their extracurricular activities. As such, the slacker remains elusive to us, or so it appears.

Does a slacker lack personality or individuality, then? Does a slacker suffer from an existential crisis? One way a slacker may address this concern is by expanding alternate ways to *be*. Perhaps the what-do-you-do question is not the right question to begin with. The slacker may say, "Sure. The things we do can inform who we are—but there are other things relevant to who we are." In addition to their work, we may also gain a sense of who someone is by learning about their family history, political stances, moral commitments, or even their hopes and fears. There are things other than work that are constitutive of who we are. For instance, some may define themselves by their possessions: "I am the guy who owns a gold toilet." Some may define themselves by their beliefs: "I am an atheist." Some may define themselves by their attitudes, "I am an optimist." Some may define themselves by their trauma, "I am a survivor." And some may even define themselves by their relationship, "I am a cat-parent."

Let's explore further the kind of identity that is forged by one's relationships. A slacker may not have a lot to offer if someone asks them "What do you do?" But the same slacker may have a lot more to say if asked about their family or relationships that are significant to them. It is not uncommon for people to identify themselves with parenthood, for example. (Former First Lady of the United States, Michelle Obama, is a self-declared "mom-in-chief."[6]) Kinship, not just work or achievements, can also give us a sense of who we are. In fact, having a significant relationship often brings clarity about the kind of person one is. A new parent may learn that they can love another person even more than they love themselves—something the parent may not have known about themselves before having the child.

Admittedly, relationships are entangled with work in at least two important ways. First, a relationship takes work. Maintaining a relationship is laborious. For instance, keeping a good relationship with my cat linguini requires coming home before she wakes up from her afternoon nap, grading papers in an awkward position to accommodate her sleeping on my lap, and scouting around for a variety of treats. One may argue that, since a relationship often comes with responsibilities, defining oneself in terms of one's relationships is just a more oblique way to define oneself with work. In other words, we cannot avoid perceiving ourselves through the lens of work.

Nevertheless, a slacker is not someone who never works. It's just that they don't work *for the purpose* of making themselves useful. Similarly, the work that we do for those we care about has little to do with making ourselves useful (at least, it needn't be). I care for linguini not because it makes me a better version of myself. Even if I do feel useful or worthy by serving linguini, my feeling of usefulness or worthiness is simply a side effect, rather than the purpose of my service to her. If I get out of bed in the middle of the night to clean up after linguini, that doesn't mean that I "identify" myself as someone who cleans up cat puke, nor does it mean that I see myself predominantly as my cat's caretaker. There are other ways I relate to linguini that don't involve work or labor. In other words, even in a labor-intensive relationship, it is still the *relationship*, rather than the labor, that is constitutive of who we are.

There is a second way that relationships are entangled with work. It is not uncommon to hear someone declare that an important person has made them "a better person." Often that means someone has motivated an individual to pull themselves together: to be more useful or purposeful, to be a better version of themselves. Perhaps a new parent is working harder because they want to take good care of their firstborn; perhaps a new romantic interest has brought out the competitive, ambitious spirit of a former slacker; or perhaps an individual strives to be better because they want to be worthy of their loved one. But in such cases, the striving is merely a function of the relationship, rather than a necessary component of it. Suppose a former slacker turns into a go-getter after the birth of their first child. It doesn't necessarily mean that the former slacker would all of a sudden identify themselves with their work. Rather, as long as it is the relationship that motivates the striving, it is more likely that the former slacker would define themselves in terms of their relationship. A former slacker is more likely to say, "I am a Dad," than "I am an employee of the month."

Since our identity can be forged in many different ways, the fact that the slacker doesn't do much needn't pose an existential threat. While a slacker may address the alleged crisis of their "being" by challenging the primacy of "doing," I suggest that a more fitting response from a slacker is simply to shrug their shoulders. Suppose the slacker concedes that being is linked to doing. Suppose the slacker also concedes that their being is in jeopardy because of their lack of doing. What might follow from such concessions? In Chapter 6, we saw the strategy O'Conner uses to address the worthiness issue. The worthiness issue, recall, is the concern that the idler's lack of effort to make themselves useful makes them unworthy of who they are (as a rational being). O'Conner does not attempt to redefine worthiness to help the idlers fit in. Rather, he questions the relevance of worthiness for the idlers. In O'Conner's reading, Kant never quite succeeds in explaining why the idler should *care* about being worthy or making an effort, other than appealing to our rational nature.[7] Yet, as O'Conner also points out, if striving to better ourselves is already in our nature, why would it even be necessary to persuade the idler to try to be worthy?[8] More importantly, if a life of idleness has been working out for the idler, what is there to be gained by the idler changing the way they live?[9]

Might the slacker offer the same response to concerns over the "crisis" of their being? Much like the idler is unconcerned with their worthiness (or the lack thereof), the slacker may also be indifferent to the question of being. We can imagine the slacker shrugging their shoulders, saying, "Why do I need to know who I am? What do I care if you don't know who I am?"[10] Indeed, why would the slacker be concerned about their "being" all of a sudden? If "not doing" has not created an existential crisis for the slacker before, why would it be a problem *now*? So, perhaps the more true-to-a-slacker response to the question of being is just to say, "Why should I care?" Instead of resolving the issues of their worthiness and their "being," the slacker *dissolves* these issues by denying their relevance. The slacker simply goes with the flow; their existence is contoured by strolling along the path of least resistance.

* * *

The idea that we need to live up to who we are through work is not unique to Kant. It is in fact the credo of our productivity culture. Interestingly, even pro-leisure thinkers subscribe to the significance of living up to who we are. As I argued in Chapter 1, several pro-leisure thinkers consider anti-industriousness a necessary means of achieving an authentic mode of human existence. This authentic mode of existence comes in different flavors: be it autonomy, human dignity, self-actualization, or resistance to conventional notions of success.[11] By valorizing leisure (or not working) as the true path to who we are or ought to be, these thinkers ascribe existential significance to leisure. Nevertheless, in their efforts to defend leisure, these thinkers also inadvertently *instrumentalize* it. One contemporary example of such instrumentalization is Richard Linklater's film *Slacker*. As we saw in Chapter 2, the slackers in Linklater's story are participants in a countercultural movement, and slacking is presented as a critique of capitalism. But here's the irony: as soon as we turn leisure into a liberatory force, it ceases to be laid-back and carefree. As soon as we turn slackers into dissenters or cultural critics, they are no longer purposeless.

Furthermore, pro-work and pro-leisure thinkers may have more in common than they care to admit. First, our pro-leisure thinkers insist that not working is the way to *be*—much like pro-work thinkers insist that work is the way to *be*. By substituting "work" with "not working," our pro-leisure thinkers have merely negated what the pro-work thinkers take to be existentially important. Instead of work, our pro-leisure thinkers say, not-work. But even the negation of work is still operating within the same paradigm of work. That is, the pro-leisure thinkers continue to conceptualize being through the lens of labor (or, in their case, the lack thereof). But as we have seen, work is just one of the many ways we conceive of ourselves as individuals. Our relationships, beliefs, and commitments also make us who we are in addition to our work. Ironically, by prioritizing their effort to negating work, pro-leisure thinkers implicitly affirm that there is something special about the status of work.

Second, both the pro-work and pro-leisure thinkers believe that there is a particular way to be and that it is encumbered upon us to live up to it. As such, while they disagree on what that particular way to be looks like, neither group questions the primacy of being.[12] In Chapter 6, I argued that the demand to be worthy is just a different iteration of the demand to maximize our potential or talents. Instead of saying, "given your aptitude in physics, you could have a promising career in academia and so you ought to go to graduate school," Kant says, "given your rationality, you could rise above a mere animal and so you ought to live a life worthy of who you are." The demand for us to cultivate our talents is at the service of our worthiness. Interestingly, pro-leisure thinkers are making a similar move here. Whereas pro-work thinkers such as Kant believe that we need to make something of ourselves in order to live up to who we are, pro-leisure thinkers have simply substituted work with leisure as the means to a more authentic, liberated self. Instead of cultivating our talents, our pro-leisure thinkers tell us that not working is what allows us to *be* or live up to who we are. As such, even for the pro-leisure thinkers, the achievement of proper personhood is still a goal for which we strive.

Leisure is the new work. Not working is the new doing. In their attempt to canonize leisure as the foundation of an authentic life, pro-leisure thinkers miss an opportunity to challenge the expectation to "live up to who we are." For many, the demand to live up to our potential seems so obvious that no defense is needed. However, the slacker calls into question (albeit unintentionally) this very obviousness. That is, they call into question the demand to maximize, or even develop, our talents. They call into question the demand to be a "useful" individual. They call into question the demand to strive to be one's best. Clearly, the slacker is not compelled to follow the script set by our status-obsessed, hyper-productive culture.

With this in mind, it is more than a little puzzling that pro-leisure thinkers would make the same assumptions as their pro-work counterparts. That is, both sides imagine that there is a specific way for us to live that allows us to do justice to who we are. For the pro-work thinkers, we need to make ourselves useful in order to be worthy. For the pro-leisure thinkers, we need to engage in leisure in order to self-actualize, or be authentic, or be autonomous. But must there be any standard for which we strive? (Even if striving involves "not working" in the case of the pro-leisure thinkers.) What is our fascination with being worthy, authentic, or free? What are we trying to prove? And to whom? Surely someone who rebels against productivity culture need not prove themselves to anyone. If we admire the slacker for their lack of compulsion to play by the script, then it is foolish of us to make slacking the new script for authenticity. Regrettably, pro-leisure thinkers have liberated us from the toxicity of hyper-productivity culture only to have us subjugated again. This time, instead of the tyranny of work, we are held hostage by the ever-elusive ideal of authenticity.

The slacker bewilders many of us in part because they challenge our entrenched belief that we are what we do. Given that we have been raised in a culture where our work determines our identity and worth, it is not at all surprising that we don't quite know what to make of slackers. So, what happens when we disengage doing from being? What happens when we no longer define ourselves by what we do? Is it even possible? I've argued that when it comes to forging our identity and self-worth, there are alternatives to work—relationships being one example. If we can expand ways to understand who we are, if work is not the only thing that defines us, then a slacker may not be so elusive after all.

In the concluding chapter, I will further examine the slacker's attitude of indifference. If a slacker is indifferent to the matter of their own worthiness and is uninterested in following any life script, would they even care to *defend* themselves? Indeed, would a slacker even be interested in reading this book?

The Pandemic Slacker

A good portion of this book was written during lockdown when the COVID-19 pandemic upended the world that we knew. All of a sudden, instead of interacting with my students in the classroom, I found myself talking at them through a screen. Instead of deciphering philosophical texts, I found myself trying to make sense of statistical data in graphs, maps, and charts. Things that were once harmless became dangerous: doorknobs, keys, the air we breathe. Behaviors that were once innocent became suspect: a sneeze, a cough, a handshake. Given the strange time in which we live, I find myself asking: Should I be writing a defense on slackers now? On the one hand, it seems absurd to continue a book project as if our lives were untouched by the pandemic. When so many people have lost their jobs, when so many people are forced to do nothing, a defense of slacking seems out of touch, perhaps even insensitive. On the other hand, the project provides a sort of refuge, a normalcy that says, "not everything has to succumb to this pandemic." So, I did a bit of a compromise and started to reflect on what it means to be a slacker (or go-getter) during a pandemic. What does it mean to be a slacker during a pandemic? What does the pandemic tell us about our work and productivity cultures?

At first glance, the pandemic seems to encourage slacking. The "pandemic slackers" see the opportunity to stay home as a license to slack. Streaming services for movies and TV shows saw a significant increase in usage and new subscriptions during the pandemic. Netflix, for example, added 15.8 million subscribers in the first quarter of 2020, twice as many as the company projected.[1] A quick search on the internet yields countless lists recommending binge-worthy shows specifically designed for people who now find too much time on their hands. Before the shelter-in-place order took effect in California, there were long lines outside of marijuana dispensaries.[2] Meanwhile, underground weed delivery services report a significant increase in demand. According to the owner of a cannabis delivery service, they are getting twice as much business as normal—"Every day is a Friday."[3] All of a sudden, many of us turned into the classic Hollywood slacker that we saw in Chapter 3: the pot-smoking couch potato who watches TV all day. It seems that being forced to stay at home has brought out the inner slacker from many of us.

The counterparts of the pandemic slackers are the "pandemic go-getters." Like a pandemic slacker, a pandemic go-getter sees the lockdown as an opportunity. Unlike the pandemic slacker, however, the pandemic go-getter uses this opportunity for self-improvement. They are the ones who commence rigorous at-home workouts, sign up for courses on MasterClass, try their hands at fermenting, bake their own bread, and build their own chicken coop and raise chickens. Pandemic go-getters don't just try to kill time, they try to be useful. For every list of "best movies to stream during your quarantine" on the internet for the slackers, there is an online article devoted to pandemic projects for the go-getters. So many people have taken up baking at home that flour and yeast were in short supply across the United States.[4] As such, the pandemic also reinforces our hyper-productivity culture.

While the pandemic has given license for some to slack, it has also brought out the inner go-getters from many of us.

Our ambivalence surrounding work is evidenced by the contradictory commentaries on productivity that inundates us. We see *both* strategies on how to remain productive *and* commentaries on why we shouldn't expect ourselves to be productive during the pandemic. On the productivity side, *Time* magazine suggests "5 tips for staying productive and mentally healthy while you're working from home,"[5] NPR gives us "8 Tips To Make Working From Home Work For You,"[6] and *Vogue* magazine is an overachiever, offering "11 Tips for Working From Home—Without Losing Your Mind."[7] On the counter-productivity side, we have articles such as "Stop trying to be productive,"[8] "There is no such thing as 'productivity' during a pandemic,"[9] and "It's OK if you are not being productive during the COVID 19 pandemic,"[10] just to name a few. Interestingly, some of these anti-productivity commentaries seem to advocate a slacker attitude by highlighting the importance of "getting by." One author writes, "It is just enough to get by, if that's all you're capable of, since 'getting by' may be the new emotional normal for months to come."[11] Another advises, "focus less about figuring out a detailed strategy for how to be as happy and productive as possible, and more on just getting through the day."[12] Notice, however, the kind of "getting by" these commentators advocate is not the same as the kind of "getting by" we see in slackers. For these authors, the reason we are allowed to be content with getting by during a pandemic is not that we are indifferent to success or accomplishment, like the slackers we encounter in this book. Rather, it's OK for us to set a low bar now because we are too exhausted to go above and beyond, and legitimately so. Being able to get by is actually the *best* we could do right now.

The anti-productivity commentators are not advocating for slacking as much as they are advocating for a sustainable way of coping. We "slack" because we know our limits and we take care of ourselves.

The surge in commentaries on how to stay productive is in part a function of workers being forced to work from home, as many companies have closed their offices to help curb the spread of the virus. Many of us have to reconfigure our home into a workplace, both physically and mentally. The living room where we used to watch TV and relax after work is now doubled as an office, a conference room, a daycare center, a classroom, or a combination of some or all of the above. Not only do we have to make the physical space conducive to work, but we also have to adjust ourselves mentally so that when we walk into the living room, we don't automatically look for the TV remote. A personal side-note: one day when an emergency construction project took place right outside my building in the middle of a Zoom class, I had to relocate to the furthest room away from the windows, which happened to be my bathroom. Thankfully, Zoom's virtual background helped me conceal the fact that I was delivering a lecture on Kantian deontology while sitting on a toilet. Of course, with mass layoffs and an unemployment rate rivaling the Great Depression in the United States, even having to teach on a toilet is a privilege. And when essential workers are risking their lives and health to supply our basic necessities, being able to work from home is a luxury that many do not have. Nevertheless, the blurring of the home/work boundaries is a striking reminder that we are now *always* at work, despite being away from the office or campus. Ironically, losing a physical space where we work makes it even harder to get out of work.

Those who are fortunate enough to be able to work remotely have to adapt to the new reality that they are now always at work. Meanwhile, people who are forced out of their job have to deal with the new reality that they are no longer working. In the United States, 20.5 million jobs were lost in April 2020 alone; and over 40 million US workers filed for unemployment benefits between March and May 2020. Food banks saw an unprecedented increase in need. One food bank based in Las Vegas was spending an extra $300,000 to $400,000 a week to buy food.[13] Another food bank in San Antonio doubled the number of people it was feeding: from 60,000 pre-pandemic to 120,000 people in May 2020.[14] The imminence of hunger is devastating in and of itself. But for many, there is also a psychological hurdle to overcome. Many people going to the food drives had never been unemployed until now, and they have to seek help for the first time.[15] Their anxiety is palpable. For some, having to ask for food has shaken their idea of the American dream. One immigrant from Romania told the reporter, "'When I came to America [...] I never thought I would need [welfare].'"[16] For others, having to ask for help undermines their sense of self-sufficiency. One food drive volunteer recalls that many people "tried to explain themselves" by telling her that they did have a job and that they had never done anything like this before—in the hope of showing her that "they weren't takers."[17]

The fear of being viewed as a "taker" is indicative of the anxiety surrounding welfare. There is a long-standing myth in the United States that people on welfare are lazy, parasitic, and freeloading. Could the pandemic change the perception that people on welfare are not trying hard enough? Is such a myth sustainable if one in four American workers become unemployed all at once? Of course, an empirical fact is not always effective when it comes to altering one's deeply held beliefs, biases, and prejudices. A diehard anti-welfarist may insist that those who lost their job should still try to find employment: they could get trained to be a contact tracer; they could take advantage of the COVID-19 hiring spree from companies such as Amazon and Wal-Mart; they could do side gigs such as delivering food or shopping for groceries. Nevertheless, with such a high unemployment rate, most people probably know someone who is unemployed due to the pandemic, even if they are fortunate enough to keep their job. Surely, some of the newly unemployed individuals they know would not fit the stereotype of a lazy freeloader. Suppose one's hard-working, bootstrapping uncle had to apply for food stamps and wait in line for a hot meal because he had lost his job, would one still insist that welfare is only for lazy "takers"? Of course, one may hold onto their belief by insisting that those whom they know to be hard-working are the exceptions and that welfare programs on the whole still enable free-loaders and disincentivize working. Nevertheless, the sudden and dramatic spike in unemployment makes it clear that "not working" is different from slacking or being lazy. It may then help de-stigmatize those who ask for assistance. As a man in Minnesota who recently lost his job acknowledged, he had to "set aside his deeply felt conviction that people who had to seek the aid [...] weren't trying hard enough."[18]

Of course, divorcing the unemployed from the slackers doesn't make a case for slacking. It defends those who are not working due to circumstances beyond their control, but it doesn't defend slackers, who seem to be willfully lazy. Even if the pandemic can help change the way Americans think about welfare programs, slacking (or not "trying hard enough") is still frowned upon. Even if the diehard anti-welfarist has a change of heart about unemployment benefits, they still have no reason to endorse slacking. So, separating not working from slacking doesn't seem to do much for the slackers. But as we will see, in a rather surprising twist, the couch potato slacker became a symbol of patriotism in our ever-evolving pandemic narratives.

PATRIOTIC SLACKERS

In late March 2020, when most of the United States was in lockdown, a meme that made its round on social media read, "Your grandparents were called to war. You're being called to sit on your couch. You can do this." Around the same time, British broadcaster Piers Morgan expressed a similar sentiment in a rant during his show, *Good Morning Britain*, "You're not having to risk your life in the trenches, you're being asked to go home and watch telly."[19] Harry Fenn, a 95-year-old World War II veteran in Britain published a video on Facebook in which he urged youngsters to stay at home: "In 1944, I served my country and did my duty. Now it's your duty to sit on the couch. Please save lives. It's as simple as that."[20] American actor and comedian Larry David made a public service announcement urging people to stay home using a similar language:

I basically want to address the idiots out there, and you know who you are […] You're hurting old people like me. Well, not me, I have nothing to do with you, I'll never see you. But other, let's say, other old people who might be your relatives, who the hell knows? The problem is you're passing up a fantastic opportunity, a once in a lifetime opportunity to stay in the house, sit on the couch and watch TV […] Go home, watch TV, that's my advice to you.[21]

Interestingly, David invokes the elderly here not to inspire our patriotism, but to appeal to our empathy. Though David doesn't compare sitting on one's couch to sacrificing for one's country, he calls upon our civic duty to care for the elderly, a population particularly vulnerable to the virus. So even though there is no patriotic overtone to his plea, he is still asking us to "do our part." It is noteworthy that none of these appeals simply say, "stay home," or "stay home and write your novel," or "stay home and workout." We are asked to "sit on the couch" and "watch telly." The slacker stereotype is specifically invoked to highlight how little we are being asked to do. The idea behind the meme, Morgan's rant, the veteran's plea, and David's public service announcement is simple: all that one is asked to do to "sacrifice" for one's country or loved ones is to stay home and take it easy. Do your part, be a slacker.

The juxtaposition of war and the pandemic is not new. As many have observed, we use war metaphors extensively to describe our experiences in the pandemic.[22] President Trump declared himself a "war-time president"; healthcare professionals are "frontline" workers; patients are in a "battle" with the virus, just to name a few. Commentators have cited the problematic assumptions and implications of such war metaphors. For example, unlike soldiers, health care professionals did not enter into the profession with the expectation that they would be risking their (and their family's) lives.[23] Comparing a pandemic to war may promote the idea that deaths are mere "collateral damage" or that they are "inevitable."[24] Furthermore, war metaphors often invite an "inward-looking, my-country-first attitude," an attitude that typifies nationalism.[25]

Despite the prevalent use of war metaphors in pandemic narratives, it is still striking that slacking by staying home becomes a call of duty. After all, "slacker" was a pejorative term widely used in a military context. In the United States during World War I, the term "slacker" initially referred to individuals who evaded military service or failed to contribute to the war effort. A 1918 *New York Times* article titled "Net for Slackers to Be Nation-Wide" described a national effort to round up draft evaders, as "officials are determined that less patriotic men shall not be permitted to escape."[26] Around the same time, under the heading, "Douse Slacker in Paint," *Sausalito News* reported that a man named Andy Tomko was doused in red paint when he refused to make a contribution to the Red Cross war fund.[27] The word "slacker" even referred to idle materials or objects that could have been used for the war effort. For example, unused records and record players were collected for soldiers overseas to boost morale during the "Slacker Record Week," "a movement to force slacker records to do some substantial work for the country."[28] To be a slacker is to be unpatriotic—in 1918.

Remarkably, the term "slacker" was central to the mask-wearing campaign during the 1918 pandemic. The following passage from the Hasting Center Bioethics Briefing is telling,

> Given that the 1918 pandemic coincided with a time of war and heightened patriotism, Americans were particularly inclined to heed governmental mandates. When the pandemic hit the United States in September 1918, the term "slacker," originally applied to those who refused to support the war effort, was quickly applied to people who protested public health edicts.[29]

During the pandemic, the term "slacker" was extended to those who refused to wear a mask. Under the heading "A Gauze Mask is 99% Proof Against Influenza," a Red Cross poster reads, "Doctors wear them. Those who do not wear them get sick. The man or woman or child who will not wear a mask now is a dangerous slacker."[30] In San Francisco, "mask-slackers" were arrested and fined on the charge of "disturbing the peace,"[31] much like vigilante groups were organizing "slacker raids" across the countries to round up young men without draft cards. That the term "slacker" was used in both the military and pandemic contexts is striking. It implies that mask-slackers are not just a public health hazard, but also unpatriotic. They are "disturbers of peace" in their own city while their country is at war. The intersection of mask-wearing and patriotism was partly strategic. At the time, a lot of men were disinclined to wear a mask because mask-wearing was perceived as feminine and weak. To counter this perception, public health education began to promote mask-wearing as an expression of patriotism and discipline.[32] And those who didn't wear a mask were deemed "slackers"—traitors to their country, on par with war evaders.

In the 2020 pandemic, mask-wearing once again becomes the site where one's patriotism is on display, and also where one's masculinity is contested. In May 2020, former vice president Joe Biden (then the presumptive Democratic presidential candidate) made his first public appearance at a Memorial Day ceremony after two months of quarantining at home. Memorial Day is of course laden with patriotic sentiment; and when Biden showed up with a mask on, his mask-wearing instantly took on a patriotic overtone. Meanwhile, President Trump has resisted mask-wearing, even after the Centers for Disease Control and Prevention (CDC) implored Americans to wear a face covering in public. President Trump jumped at the opportunity to undermine Biden, sharing a tweet that appeared to mock Biden's mask-wearing.[33] Such resistance to mask-wearing recalls the toxic masculinity that fueled the anti-mask-wearing sentiment from 1918. As one of Trump's supporters says, mask-wearing is "submission, it's muzzling yourself, it looks weak— especially for men."[34]

Thankfully, our treatment of slackers nowadays is less militant. While some do believe that we owe it to society to make ourselves useful (as we saw in Chapter 6), it is not usually couched in the language of patriotism. There is no slacker raid on campus rounding up students who don't pull their weight on their group project, or professors who don't show up at their department meetings. No student is fined for turning in mediocre papers; no professor is arrested for not publishing in top-tier journals. But this is largely a function of how the term itself has evolved. The war-slackers and mask-slackers were unwilling to do their share, be it defending one's country or curbing a deadly infectious disease. As long as they were deemed irresponsible and selfish, they at least deserved a reprimand.

But the slackers that I defend in this book are quite different. As I argued throughout the book, slackers are underachievers who are indifferent to self-betterment or conventional notions of success. They don't care to make something of themselves, but they still do their share of the work. If there were a draft right now, a slacker would register and report to duty. But they won't have the ambition to advance in rank, nor would they care to make a career out of being in the military. The recruiting slogan of the US Army in the 1980s and 1990s, "Be all you can be," means little to them. A slacker in the 2020 pandemic may very well wear their mask and wash their hands. Yet a slacker would never treat a quarantine or lockdown as an opportunity to write a book, learn a new language, or start a podcast. They were unmotivated to improve themselves pre-pandemic, and they are not going to start now.

Admittedly, the plea for youngsters to "sit on the couch to watch telly" is snarky and a little patronizing. However, given the history of the word "slacker" in the military context, it is nothing short of remarkable that we are now called to our duty to be a slacker. Whereas patriotism in 1918 meant wearing a mask or dying for one's country, patriotism in 2020 means sitting on one's couch. Given the hustle culture we have nowadays, being able to do nothing may very well be an accomplishment. And given that we have been ingrained with an on-the-go mentality, staying home and sitting on our couch can be a feat of self-discipline. The idea that slacking is an act of patriotism brings us back to the two recurring themes in this book: 1) the instrumentalization of leisure/idleness/not working and 2) the connection between being and doing.

First, as I argued in Chapter 1, when pro-leisure philosophers advocate for leisure/idleness/not working, they end up instrumentalizing it. For Russell and Pieper, leisure is at the service of civilization and progress. For Shippen, it is true leisure (rather than commodified pseudo-leisure) that enables us to engage in meaningful, reflective, self-actualizing activities. For Lin, O'Conner, and Cohen, idling or not working functions as a protest, a deliberate choice to reject material wealth and conventional ideas of success. For every one of these pro-leisure thinkers, leisure is a path to a more authentic form of freedom or mode of being. Today, slacking in pandemic narratives seems to serve a similar purpose. In a pandemic, we are not slacking for its own sake, but for the greater good, be it the good of our country or the protection of vulnerable citizens.

It seems that even in a pandemic, we couldn't help but assign a higher purpose to sitting on one's couch and watching TV.

But slacking—at least the version I have been defending—is resistant to the kind of instrumentalization that I have traced in other pro-leisure writings. The kind of slacker that I defend is not a slacker with a cause. After all, slackers are characterized by their purposeless existence, their lack of compulsion to make something of themselves. A slacker just slacks. When slacking becomes a form of self-sacrifice or a symbol of patriotism, it turns into a means to an end. When slacking is made to serve a cause, it is no longer purposeless. By assigning a higher purpose to slacking, we sacrifice its uniqueness.

Second, as I argued in Chapter 7, pro-leisure thinkers replace working with leisure in our quest for who we are. Whereas our culture of productivity would have us believe that we need to work in order to *be*, our pro-leisure thinkers argue that leisure is the new work—we are most true to who we are when we are at leisure or not working. In the context of pandemic slacking, slackers become patriots. Whereas their grandfathers fought the enemy by going to the trenches, slackers fight the new, invisible enemy by sitting on their couches. Different deeds, same patriotism. By standing (or sitting) with their country, the slacker gains a sense of national identity.

The problem, however, is that a slacker is indifferent to making something of themselves. A slacker just slacks, they don't slack in *order* to be a patriot. This creates a paradox of sorts. If you do what a slacker does (sitting on your couch, watching TV) for the purpose of being patriotic, then you are not *really* a full-fledged slacker. You may act like a slacker, but you lack the indifference that defines a full-fledged slacker. Yet, if you were a full-fledged slacker and slacking is just what you do, then being a patriot is simply a side effect of your slacking. You are not slacking *to be* anything, much less a patriot. Your lifestyle may be consistent with patriotism, but that doesn't make you a patriot.

***

As the title of this book makes clear, this book offers a defense of slackers. But why defend them in the first place? Who would be interested in such a defense? And I mean being interested in a personal or existential way, not just being interested in a detached and intellectual way. (How are they different? Here's an example. I might be intellectually interested in the history of Brutalist architecture, even though I am not personally, or existentially, invested in the topic. I am, however, existentially interested in the topic of feline social behavior, given that it informs how I should relate to my cat, as well as the kind of caretaker I ought to be.) So, who might be invested in a defense of slackers? Who are the stakeholders when it comes to a debate on slacking?

At first glance, a slacker may seem like an obvious answer to both questions. A slacker is undoubtedly an important stakeholder. Given that this book offers a defense of slacking, some may even think that this is a book written for the slacker. However, as I hope this book has made clear, a slacker doesn't always subscribe to conventional values. After all, they feel no compulsion to make something of themselves, despite living in a society that puts a premium on usefulness and productivity. Accordingly, they don't necessarily concern themselves with the type of questions that most consider important. For example, in Chapter 7, I argued that a slacker may be indifferent to the question of being, just like O'Conner's idler is indifferent to the question of worthiness. Instead of addressing an alleged existential crisis in some clever ways, a slacker may not even concede that there is a crisis to begin with.

Given the slacker's unconventional value system, it seems unwise for us to presume that the slacker is gung-ho about defending their way of living. In fact, a slacker may not feel compelled to defend themselves at all. If someone admonishes a slacker for slacking, they will probably just shrug their shoulders and go back to playing their video game. (This is why slackers can be so infuriating.) So, even if they could use the arguments offered in this book to defend their apathetic attitude toward being useful, they may not be motivated to deploy them. So, what's the point of mounting a defense, if the "defendant" is not even interested in defending themselves? Well, what about the non-slackers? Might this book inspire the non-slackers to live a more carefree life?

As I argued in the Introduction, the goal of this book is modest. I do not seek to *advocate* slacking, but merely to defend it. My reasoning is twofold. First, it is difficult to advocate slacking without assigning some higher purpose to it. The pro-leisure thinkers whom we have met in this book all try to make leisure a preferable way of living. And by doing so, they all end up instrumentalizing leisure. That is, they all end up making leisure *useful* in some way. But why should we insist that leisure or slacking is a preferable way of living in the first place? Whom are we trying to convert? If you were already a slacker, you don't need conversion. And if you weren't a slacker, it is unlikely that you could become one just by reading an argument.

This brings us to my second reason: it is difficult to be evangelical about slacking because it is not just a way of living, but also an attitude. One could model after a slacker by doing stereotypical slacker things: smoking pot in your friend's basement, watching TV all day, turning in a mediocre term paper, and so on. But an apathetic attitude toward one's success, or a lack of interest in fulfilling one's potential, is not something that one could simply imitate. For a slacker, slacking is not a deliberate choice or an act of resistance—it is purposeless and effortless. A slacker is not interested in making something of themselves or trying to be anyone. They slack simply because they don't care to make themselves useful. So, even if I made a foolproof argument in favor of slacking, an attitude of indifference is not something one could adopt at the flick of a switch. The faux slacker and the disingenuous slacker we encountered earlier both try to *act* like a slacker by pretending that they are too cool to care. But as I argued in Chapter 2, the faux slacker tries to cover up their hard work to make their accomplishments look effortless, while the disingenuous slacker flaunts their effortless accomplishments to impress others. Neither the faux slacker nor the disingenuous slacker is truly indifferent toward their accomplishments, as long as both of them are seeking external validation to their success. In other words, even if a slacker is imitable in appearance, they are not imitable in spirit.

Might this book offer some solace to those who care about the slacker, such as the slacker's parents or professors? Perhaps some disappointed parents will pick up this book at the bookstore one day when they feel like they are at their wit's end with their 30-year-old living in their basement. The slacker's parents are understandably invested in the slacker's well-being, especially the slacker's moral character. For example, the parents may wonder, "We have a slacker child. Does it mean our child is selfish and irresponsible? Have we raised a bad person?" In this book, I argued that being selfish and irresponsible are not the essential qualities of a slacker. If the slacker's parents find the argument persuasive, then it would offer them some relief. It may also be reassuring to know that they have not failed parenthood by raising a selfish freeloader. In short, a defense of slackers may help those who care about the slacker cope with their anxiety. This, I hope, is what this book was able to accomplish.

I will now end this book, seeing that it has finally reached the word count required by my contract.

Notes

INTRODUCTION

1. Weber, *The Protestant Ethic and the Spirit of Capitalism*.
2. Weber, *The Protestant Ethic*, 66.
3. Weber, *The Protestant Ethic*, 67.
4. Weber, *The Protestant Ethic*, 69.
5. Aristotle, *Nicomachean Ethics*, 1103b, emphasis mine.
6. Aristotle, *Nicomachean Ethics*, 1099a.
7. Aristotle, *Nicomachean Ethics*, 1177b.
8. Headlee, *Do Nothing*; Zomorodi, *Bored and Brilliant*; Lightman, *In Praise of Wasting Time*.
9. Odell, *How to Do Nothing*.
10. Shippen, *Decolonizing Time*; Lafargue, *The Right to Be Lazy*; Mountz et al., "For Slow Scholarship"; Weeks, *The Problem with Work*.

1

1. Aristotle, *Nicomachean Ethics*, 1177b.
2. Kreider, "The Busy Trap."
3. Kreider, "The Busy Trap."
4. Kreider, "The Busy Trap."
5. In "Re-Thinking the Relation between Leisure and Freedom," Neil Carr offers a critical analysis of the relationship between leisure and freedom within modern capitalist societies. He argues that leisure as most people experience it nowadays is primarily a function of capitalism, rather than a path to personal enlightenment. The leisure industry commoditizes socially acceptable forms of leisure activities for our consumption; these commodified recreations, in turn, provide a refreshed workforce that ultimately increases productivity.

6. Tsui, "You Are Doing Something Important."

7. In "A Philosophy of Leisure," Sutherland argues for the opposite. He insists that the masses do not know how to properly enjoy leisure. Hence, "professional elite" is burdened with the responsibility to educate the average citizens. It is up to this "small groups of connoisseurs" to "create and mold taste, communicate purposes and skills, encourage the development of facilities, and accept the responsibility for cultural initiative and the development of cultural traditions" (3).

8. Russell, *In Praise of Idleness*, 13.

9. Russell, *In Praise of Idleness*, 12.

10. The distinction between passive and active pastimes is helpfully explored in Carl Newport's *Digital Minimalism*, where he argues that we need to "reclaim leisure" by prioritizing active, physically demanding activities over "passive consumption" such as flipping TV channels or scrolling through social media on our smartphones.

11. For example, reading a book to prepare for an exam is work, whereas reading a book to satisfy one's curiosity would be leisure. As such, the work-leisure distinction is better understood not in terms of the types of activity, but as differences in motivation. But even this distinction is rough. One could read *both* for preparing for an exam *and* satisfying one's curiosity. Our motivations can be different without being mutually exclusive.

12. Russell, *In Praise of Idleness*, 13.

13. Russell, *In Praise of Idleness*, 13.

14. Russell, *In Praise of Idleness*, 4.

15. Russell, *In Praise of Idleness*, 13.

16. Russell, *In Praise of Idleness*, 13.

17. Russell, *In Praise of Idleness*, 15.

18. Pieper, *Leisure*, 17.

19. Pieper, *Leisure*, 25–26.

20. Pieper, *Leisure*, 41.

21. Pieper, *Leisure*, 53.

22. Pieper, *Leisure*, 47.

23. See Hunt, "No More FOMO"; Vannucci, "Social Media Use"; Woods, "#Sleepyteens."

24. Freedom App. https://freedom.to/.

25. That Pieper and Kreider use the term "idleness" in radically different ways might have obscured the similarities of their thinking.

26. Pieper, *Leisure*, 50.

27. Pieper, *Leisure*, 52.

28. Pieper, *Leisure*, 47–48.

29. Shippen, *Decolonizing Time*, 19, emphasis in original.

30. Shippen, *Decolonizing Time*, 29.

31. Shippen, *Decolonizing Time*, 28.

32. See Owens's "Aristotle on Leisure" for a helpful discussion regarding the differences between leisure and entertainment.

33. Shippen, *Decolonizing Time*, 70.

34. Shippen, *Decolonizing Time*, 19.

35. Shippen, *Decolonizing Time*, 18.

36. Shippen, *Decolonizing Time*, 20.

37. Lin, *The Importance of Living*, 149. Like Russell, Lin also uses "idle," "leisure," "lazy," and "loafing" interchangeably.

38. Lin, *The Importance of Living*, 151.

39. Lin, *The Importance of Living*, 151.

40. This attitude recalls the fable "The Fox and the Grapes" from one of Aesop's fables. After repeated attempts to reach for the grapes failed, the fox decided that the grapes must be sour and that he didn't really want them anyway. Much like the fox who imagined the grapes to be sour, these Chinese scholars imagined the life of a civil servant undesirable. They began to adapt a preference for a different way of life—the life of idleness.

41. Lin, *The Importance of Living*, 152.

42. Lin, *The Importance of Living*, 152.

43. Tao also went by "Tao Chien."

44. See Davis, "The Character of a Chinese Scholar-Official," 39.

45. Tao, "Homecoming"; "幼稚盈室，缾無儲粟," my translation.

46. Tao, "Homecoming"; "饑凍雖切，違己交病," my translation.

47. Lin, *The Importance of Living*, 152.

48. David Hinton's translation is, "I am not bowing down to some clod-hopper for a measly bushel of rice." See Tao, *Selected Poems*, 12.

49. Lin, *The Importance of Living*, 152.

50. O'Conner, *Idleness*, 4.

51. In fact, O'Conner explicitly states that his book is not an advocacy for idleness. Indeed, "positive recommendations risk under-appreciating how deeply an ambivalence toward idleness is constitutive of much of what many of us take ourselves to be." *Idleness*, 2.
52. O'Conner, *Idleness*, 5.
53. O'Conner, *Idleness*, 6.
54. O'Conner, *Idleness*, 19.
55. O'Conner, *Idleness*, 5.
56. O'Conner, *Idleness*, 28.
57. As I have tried to show, philosophical arguments in favor of leisure/idleness come in different flavors. It is for the sake of simplicity that I generalize these thinkers into "pro-leisure" or "anti-industriousness" categories.
58. We get our word "robot" from the Czech word for forced labor: *robota*.
59. O'Conner, *Idleness*, 172.
60. O'Conner makes a similar point in his discussion on Stevenson. He points out that the kind of idleness Stevenson defends is still at the service of self-making. *Idleness*, 171.
61. O'Conner, *Idleness*, 180.
62. O'Conner, *Idleness*, 185.
63. O'Conner, *Idleness*, 184.
64. O'Conner, *Idleness*, 185.
65. For O'Conner, in order to see idleness as a form of freedom, the idler has to own their idleness, so to speak. The idler is aware that this is the lifestyle that they have opted for. Idleness is a matter of *preference*, a *chosen* lifestyle. *Idleness*, 180.
66. O'Conner, *Idleness*, 173.
67. Cohen, *Not Working*, xii.
68. Cohen, *Not Working*, xxxiv.
69. What Cohen has in mind in particular is Pyrrhonian skepticism. A Pyrrhonian skeptic does not deny the possibility of knowledge; rather, she suspends judgment on all issues in order to achieve intellectual tranquillity.
70. Cohen, *Not Working*, 169.
71. Cohen, *Not Working*, 170.
72. Interestingly, influencers are sometimes called "Key Opinion Leaders."
73. Cohen, *Not Working*, 170.

74. Cohen, *Not Working*, 171.
75. Cohen, *Not Working*, 218.
76. Cohen, *Not Working*, 218.
77. Cohen, *Not Working*, 220.
78. O'Conner seems to want to have it both ways. On the one hand, he insists that there is no purpose to idleness; on the other hand, he insists that idleness is a deliberately chosen way of living. Can O'Conner have his cake and eat it too? That will depend on how we understand "purpose" and what role it plays (if any) when it comes to deliberating and choosing one's lifestyle. In any event, O'Conner's idlers know what they are signing up for when they *choose* idleness as a lifestyle.

2

1. Castiglione, *The Book of the Courtier*, First book.
2. Castiglione, *The Book of the Courtier*, First book.
3. Castiglione, *The Book of the Courtier*, First book.
4. O'Conner, *Idleness*, emphasis mine, 7.
5. Ratcliffe, *Oxford Essential Quotations*.
6. "Rich Kids of the Internet," Instagram account.
7. Allen, "Falling Stars Challenge."
8. Del Valle, "The #FallingStars Challenge."
9. "Slacker Script," 21–22.
10. "$23,000 film."
11. "$23,000 film," my emphasis.
12. "$23,000 film."

3

1. "Dazed and Confused Script," 10–11.
2. "Scott Pilgrim vs. the World Script," 2.
3. "Zack and Miri Make a Porno Script," 48.
4. "Office Space Script," 15.
5. "Office Space Script," 15.
6. "Office Space Script," 25.
7. "Office Space Script," 29.
8. "Office Space Script," 30.

9. "Office Space Script," 31.

10. Cohen, NotWorking, 169.

11. "Office Space Script," 65.

12. I thank one of the anonymous reviewers for the proposal for suggesting the category "slackers as rebels without a cause." Ultimately, I dropped the word "rebels"— if a slacker is slacking deliberately as a protest, then they are really dissident slackers with a cause.

13. "The Big Lebowski Script," 3.

14. "The Big Lebowski Script," 12.

15. Wall, "Two Types of Fetishism."

16. Leckrone, "Hippies, Feminists, and Neocons."

17. Kazecki, "Masculinity under (friendly) fire"; Comer, "Myth, War, Ethics."

18. "The Big Lebowski Script," 21.

19. "Clerks Script by Kevin Smith," 88.

20. "Clerks Script by Kevin Smith," 34.

21. "Clerks Script by Kevin Smith," 22.

22. "Clerks Script by Kevin Smith," 143.

23. Greene, "The Original Clerks' Ending."

24. Hoad, "How We Made Clerks."

4

1. Researchers have found that individuals use procrastination as a means to regulate short-term moods (anxiety, boredom). See Timothy Pychyl and Fuschia Sirois, "Procrastination, Emotion Regulation, and Well-Being."

2. See Locke and Schattke, "Intrinsic and Extrinsic Motivation."

3. In addition to intrinsic and extrinsic motivations, Locke and Schattke also identify achievement as an important motivation. Even if a student does not particularly enjoy the process of doing research and writing, even if the student has no one to impress, they may still be motivated by a desire to do well. Getting a good grade or knowing that they have written a good paper may itself be a source of pride, and achievement alone is a sufficient motivator for learning.

4. The estimation is likely to be too generous, given that this is a slacker student we are talking about.

5. In 2018, the news of a 30-year-old man being formally evicted by his parents briefly captured the media's attention. See Chappell, "Judge Backs N.Y. Parents."
6. McCalmont, "Walker Urges Professors to Work Harder."
7. Levy, "Do College Professors Work Hard Enough?"
8. Levy, "Do College Professors Work Hard Enough?"
9. In fact, professors spend a significant amount of time doing administrative duties. See Flaherty, "So Much to Do, So Little Time."
10. Descartes, "Meditations," 516.
11. For an example of a self-flagellating slacker professor, see MacPhail, "Productivity Is Overrated."
12. See Venkatraman, "Conventions of Scientific Authorship"; McNutt, "Transparency in Authors' Contributions."
13. Except in journals (primarily in Economics) where the order is determined alphabetically.
14. In "Beyond Authorship," Brand et al. propose a taxonomy to standardize and clarify the input of various contributors to a publication.
15. For example, The International Committee of Medical Journal Editors (ICMJE) has published a guideline with detailed recommendations on authorship. There is a long list of medical journals stating that they follow ICMJE recommendations. See http://www.icmje.org/journals-following-the-icmje-recommendations/.
16. Here's a vivid portrait of lazy professors by a student from the University of Toronto—Penn, "My Professors are Lazy."

5

1. James, "Assholes: A Theory," 5, 13.
2. James, "Assholes: A Theory," 10.
3. James, "Assholes: A Theory," 28.
4. And if they don't turn down the request, it is likely because they wish to placate others, and not because they feel an inner drive to make themselves useful.
5. Hassan, "Confronting Asian-American Stereotypes."
6. Askarinam, "Asian Americans Feel Held Back."
7. Stack, "Bravery and Nihilism."

1. Kant, 4:421 (Wood, 37). All references to *Groundwork for the Metaphysics of Morals* come from Allen Wood's translation.

2. Kant, 4:423 (Wood, 39–40).

3. Kant, 4:423 (Wood, 39–40).

4. Kant, 6:445 (Gregor, 239). All references to *Metaphysics of Morals* come from Mary Gregor's translation.

5. Kant, 6:392 (Gregor, 195).

6. Kant, 6:392 (Gregor, 195).

7. Kant, 6:387 (Gregor, 191).

8. Kant is discussing moral perfection in this quote—but it is also applicable for our purposes. Kant, 6:446 (Gregor, 241).

9. Kant, 4:423 (Wood, 39–40).

10. Kant, 6:445 (Gregor, 239).

11. Kant 4:429 (Wood, 46–47).

12. A person who commits suicide in order to "flee from a burdensome condition" is an instance of a rational being using themselves as a means to an end. Kant, 4:429 (Wood, 47).

13. Kant, 4:430 (Wood, 48).

14. James, *Assholes: A Theory*.

15. O'Conner, 46.

16. O'Conner, 46–47.

17. Kant does consider a related issue in *Metaphysics of Morals*. At one point, he discusses the possibility of someone lacking "moral endowments," such as "*moral feeling, conscience, love* of one's neighbor, and *respect* for oneself" (Kant 6:399; Gregor, 200). Kant simply denies that anyone (who is rational) would lack these moral endowments. A sociopath may lack conscience, but then they wouldn't be rational. For Kant, it is inconceivable that anyone would just not have those moral feelings. So perhaps Kant would say the same about "worthiness." That a rational being would never *not care* about the pursuit of worthiness.

18. O'Conner, 28.

1. Frankfurt also talks about the connection between being invested in (caring about) something and one's identity. In "The Importance of What We Care About," he writes, "A person who cares about

something is, as it were, invested in it. He *identifies* himself with what he cares about in the sense that he makes himself vulnerable to losses and susceptible to benefits depending upon whether what he cares about is diminished or enhanced" (260, emphasis added).

2. Adams, "To 'Be' or to 'Do,'" 323.

3. Adams, "To 'Be' or to 'Do,'" 325.

4. Adams, "To 'Be' or to 'Do,'" 326.

5. Adams, "To 'Be' or to 'Do,'" 327.

6. Obama, "Transcript: Michelle Obama Convention's Speech."

7. O'Conner, *Idleness*, 50–52.

8. O'Conner, *Idleness*, 52.

9. O'Conner, *Idleness*, 52.

10. O'Conner hints at this in his discussion of Stevenson. He points out that Stevenson's theory of idleness is yet another way to meet the challenge of self-actualization, and that he never questions the primacy of one's identity (171).

11. For Russell and Shippen, idleness (or leisure) is indispensable to the progress of civilization and the individual; for Pieper, leisure frees us from the mundane, enabling us to live with dignity; for Lin, loafing is a principled, dignified rejection of material success; for O'Conner and Cohen, idleness is a more authentic form of freedom.

12. Perhaps O'Conner's case for idleness is the outlier here, given his comments on Stevenson (see note 10). But while O'Conner may not be committed to the importance of self-making, he does present idle freedom as a more authentic form of freedom. But as I pointed out in Chapter 1, it is rather difficult to view his notion of idle freedom as value neutral, despite his claim that he is not promoting idleness.

THE PANDEMIC SLACKER

1. Alexander, "Netflix Adds Subscribers."

2. Koran, "Life under 'Shelter in Place.'"

3. Garcia, "Staying Safe."

4. Wolf, "Forget Pork"; Heil, "People Are Baking Bread"

5. Austin, "5 Tips."

6. Noguchi, "8 Tips."

7. Ruiz, "11 Tips."

8. Lorenz, "Stop Trying."

9. Millard, "There's No Such Thing."
10. Kappler, "It's OK."
11. Millard, "There's No Such Thing."
12. Kappler, "It's OK."
13. Schwartz et al., "How Bad is Unemployment?"; Kulish, "Never Seen Anything Like It."
14. Wollan. "San Antonio Food Bank."
15. Buckley, "Never Thought I Would Need It."
16. Buckley, "Never Thought I Would Need It."
17. Wollan, "San Antonio Food Bank."
18. Buckley, "Never Thought I Would Need It."
19. Speare-Cole, "Piers Morgan."
20. Keay, "World War Two Veteran Harry Fenn."
21. Legaspi, "Larry David Addresses 'Idiots Out there'"
22. See Levenson, "Calling the Coronavirus Pandemic a 'War'"; Musu, "War Metaphors Used for COVID-19"; Salles and Gold, "Comparing Health Care Workers to Soldiers"; Serhan "The Case against Waging 'War'"; Wilkinson, "Pandemics Are Not Wars."
23. Salles and Gold, "Comparing Health Care Workers to Soldiers."
24. Wilkinson, "Pandemics Are Not Wars."
25. Musu, "War Metaphors Used for COVID-19."
26. "Net for Slackers."
27. "Douse Slackers in Paint."
28. "Slacker records."
29. Stern and Markel, "Pandemics."
30. Zimmerman, "San Francisco Forced People to Wear Masks."
31. Smith, "Protesting during a Pandemic."
32. Tomes, "Destroyer and Teacher."
33. Porter, "Trump shared a tweet."
34. Hess, "The Medical Mask."

"A $23,000 Film Is Turning into a Hit." *The New York Times*, August 7, 1991. https://www.nytimes.com/1991/08/07/movies/a-23000-film-is-tu rning-into-a-hit.html.

Adams, James Truslow. "To 'Be' or to 'Do': A Note on American Education." *Forum*, June 1929, 321–27. https://www.unz.com/print/Forum-192 9jun-00321/.

Aesop. *Æsop's Fables: Illustrated by E. Griset*. London: Casell & Company, 1893.

Alexander, Julia. "Netflix Adds 15 Million Subscribers as People Stream More Than Ever, but Warns about Tough Road Ahead." *The Verge*, April 21, 2020. https://www.theverge.com/2020/4/21/21229587/netflix-ear nings-coronavirus-pandemic-streaming-entertainment.

Allen, Kerry. "Falling Stars Challenge: China's Twist on the Young Rich Millennial Meme." *BBC News*, October 25, 2018. https://www.bbc. com/news/world-asia-china-45970776.

Aristotle. *Nicomachean Ethics*. Edited by Roger Crisp. Cambridge: Cambridge University Press, 2000.

Askarinam, Leah, and National Journal. "Asian Americans Feel Held Back at Work by Stereotypes." *Atlantic*, January 26, 2016. https://www.theatlan tic.com/politics/archive/2016/01/asian-americans-feel-held-back-at-work-by-stereotypes/458874/.

Austin, Patrick Lucas. "5 Tips for Staying Productive While You're Working from Home." *Time*, March 12, 2020. https://time.com/5801725/ work-from-home-remote-tips/.

Brand, Amy, Liz Allen, Micah Altman, Marjorie Hlava, and Jo Scott. "Beyond Authorship: Attribution, Contribution, Collaboration, and Credit." *Learned Publishing* 28, no. 2 (April 1, 2015): 151–155. https://doi.org/10.1087/ 20150211.

Buckley, Cara. "'Never Thought I Would Need It': Americans Put Pride Aside to Seek Aid." *The New York Times*, March 31, 2020. https://www.nytimes.com/2020/03/31/us/virus-food-banks-unemployment.html.

Carr, Neil. "Re-Thinking the Relation between Leisure and Freedom." *Annals of Leisure Research* 20, no. 2 (2016): 137–151. https://doi.org/10.1080/11745398.2016.1206723.

Castiglione, Baldassarre. *The Book of the Courtier*. Translated by Leonard E. Opdycke. Lawrence, KS: Digireads, 2009.

Chappell, Bill. "Judge Backs N.Y. Parents, Saying Their 30-Year-Old Son Must Move Out." NPR, May 23, 2018. https://www.npr.org/sections/thetwo-way/2018/05/23/613616315/judge-backs-n-y-parents-saying-their-30-year-old-son-must-move-out.

Cohen, Josh. *Not Working: Why We Have to Stop*. London: Granta, 2018.

Comer, Todd A. "'This Aggression Will Not Stand': Myth, War, and Ethics in The Big Lebowski." *SubStance* 34, no. 2 (2005): 98–117. https://doi.org/10.1353/sub.2005.0026.

Davis, A.R. "The Character of a Chinese Scholar-Official as Illustrated by the Life and Poetry of T'Ao Yuan-Ming." *Arts: Proceedings of the Sydney University Arts Association* 1, no. 1 (1958): 37–46. https://openjournals.library.sydney.edu.au/index.php/ART/article/view/5417/6160.

Del Valle, Gaby. "The #FallingStars Challenge Highlights Extreme Wealth - and Extreme Inequality." *Vox*, October 26, 2018. https://www.vox.com/the-goods/2018/10/26/18030032/falling-stars-challenge-income-inequality.

Descartes, René. "Meditations on First Philosophy." In *Epistemology: Contemporary Readings*, edited by Michael Huemer and Robert Audi, 513–523. London: Routledge, 2008.

"Douse Slacker in Paint." *Sausalito News*, August 31, 1918. *California Digital Newspaper Collection*, UC Riverside. Accessed June 6, 2020. https://cdnc.ucr.edu/?a=d&d=SN19180831.2.32&e=-------en--20--1--txt-txIN--------1.

Flaherty, Colleen. "So Much to Do, So Little Time." *Inside HigherEd*, April 9, 2014. https://www.insidehighered.com/news/2014/04/09/research-shows-professors-work-long-hours-and-spend-much-day-meetings.

Frankfurt, Harry. "The Importance of What We Care About." *Synthese* 53, no. 2 (1982): 257–272. https://doi.org/10.1007/bf00484902.

Garcia, Sandra E. "Staying Safe While Delivering Weed in the Pandemic." *The New York Times*, April 10, 2020. https://www.nytimes.com/2020/04/10/us/weed-cannabis-delivery-coronavirus.html.

Greene, A., 2014. "Flashback: Watch The Original, Grisly Ending To 'Clerks'." *Rolling Stone*. https://www.rollingstone.com/movies/movie-news/flashback-the-original-clerks-ending-where-dante-dies-44709/

Hassan, Adeel. "Confronting Asian-American Stereotypes." *The New York Times*, June 23, 2018. https://www.nytimes.com/2018/06/23/us/confronting-asian-american-stereotypes.html.

Headlee, Celeste Anne. *Do Nothing: How to Break Away from Overworking, Overdoing, and Underliving*. New York: Harmony Books, 2020.

Heil, Emily. "People Are Baking Bread Like Crazy, and Now We're Running out of Flour and Yeast." *The Washington Post*, March 24, 2020. https://www.washingtonpost.com/news/voraciously/wp/2020/03/24/people-are-baking-bread-like-crazy-and-now-were-running-out-of-flour-and-yeast/.

Hess, Amanda. "The Medical Mask Becomes a Protest Symbol." *The New York Times*, June 2, 2020. https://www.nytimes.com/2020/06/02/arts/virus-mask-trump.html.

Hoad, Phil. "Kevin Smith: How We Made Clerks." *The Guardian*, May 7, 2019. https://www.theguardian.com/film/2019/may/07/how-we-made-clerks-kevin-smith.

Hunt, Melissa G., Rachel Marx, Courtney Lipson, and Jordyn Young. "No More FOMO: Limiting Social Media Decreases Loneliness and Depression." *Journal of Social and Clinical Psychology* 37, no. 10 (2018): 751–768. https://doi.org/10.1521/jscp.2018.37.10.751.

ICMJE. "Defining the Role of Authors and Contributors." *International Committee of Medical Journal Editors*, Accessed June 13, 2020. http://www.icmje.org/recommendations/browse/roles-and-responsibilities/defining-the-role-of-authors-and-contributors.html#two.

James, Aaron. *Assholes: A Theory*. New York: Anchor, 2014.

Kant, Immanuel. *The Metaphysics of Morals*. Translated by Mary Gregor. Cambridge: Cambridge University Press, 1991.

Kant, Immanuel. *Groundwork for the Metaphysics of Moral*. Edited and Translated by Allen W. Wood. New Haven, CT: Yale University Press, 2002.

Kappler, Maija. "It's OK If You're Not 'Making the Most Of' This Pandemic." *HuffPost Canada*, April 16, 2020. https://www.huffingtonpost.ca/entry/

coronavirus-productivity-mental-health_ca_5e80e5c7c5b6cb9dc
1a22d88.

Kazecki, Jakub. "'What Makes a Man, Mr. Lebowski?': Masculinity under
(Friendly) Fire in Ethan and Joel Coen's The Big Lebowski." *Atenea* 28,
no. 1 (June 2008): 147–159.

Keay, Lara. "Jersey D-Day World War Two Veteran Harry Fenn Makes
Emotional Plea to Young Sit on the Couch." *Daily Mail Online*, March 25,
2020. https://www.dailymail.co.uk/news/article-8150519/Jersey-D-
Day-World-War-Two-veteran-Harry-Fenn-makes-emotional-plea-youn
g-sit-couch.html.

Koran, Mario. "Life under 'Shelter in Place': Long Lines, Empty Roads,
Panic-Buying Cannabis." *The Guardian*, March 17, 2020. https://www.
theguardian.com/world/2020/mar/17/life-under-shelter-in-place-l
ong-lines-empty-roads-panic-buying-cannabis.

Kreider, Tim. "The 'Busy' Trap." *The New York Times*, June 30, 2012. https://op
inionator.blogs.nytimes.com/2012/06/30/the-busy-trap/.

Kulish, Nicholas. "'Never Seen Anything Like It': Cars Line Up for Miles
at Food Banks." *The New York Times*, April 8, 2020. https://www.nytimes.
com/2020/04/08/business/economy/coronavirus-food-banks.html.

Lafargue, Paul. *The Right to Be Lazy: Essays by Paul Lafargue*. Edited by Bernard
Marszalek. Oakland, CA: AK Press, 2011.

Leckrone, J. Wesley. "Hippies, Feminists, and Neocons: Using the Big
Lebowski to Find the Political in the Nonpolitical." *PS: Political Science &
Politics* 46, no. 1 (2013): 129–136. https://doi.org/10.1017/s10490
96512001321.

Legaspi, Althea. "Larry David Addresses the 'Idiots Out There' in California
Coronavirus PSA." *Rolling Stone*, March 31, 2020. https://www.rollings
tone.com/tv/tv-news/larry-david-california-coronavirus-psa-976300/.

Levenson, Eric. "Officials Keep Calling the Coronavirus Pandemic a 'War.'
Here's Why." *CNN*, April 2, 2020. https://www.cnn.com/2020/04/01/
us/war-on-coronavirus-attack/index.html.

Levy, David C. "Do College Professors Work Hard Enough?" *The Washington
Post*, March 23, 2012. https://www.washingtonpost.com/opinions/do-
college-professors-work-hard-enough/2012/02/15/gIQAn058VS_
story.html.

Lightman, Alan. *In Praise of Wasting Time*. New York: TED Books, 2018.

Lin, Yutang. *The Importance of Living*. New York: Willam Morrow, 1998.

Locke, Edwin A., and Kaspar Schattke. "Intrinsic and Extrinsic Motivation: Time for Expansion and Clarification." *Motivation Science* 5, no. 4 (2019): 277–290. https://doi.org/10.1037/mot0000116.

Lorenz, Taylor. "Stop Trying to Be Productive." *The New York Times*, April 1, 2020. https://www.nytimes.com/2020/04/01/style/productivity-coronavirus.html.

MacPhail, Theresa. "OK, I Admit It: Productivity Is Overrated." *Chronicle of Higher Education*, July 29, 2019. https://www.chronicle.com/article/OK-I-Admit-It-Productivity/246744.

McCalmont, Lucy. "Walker Urges Professors to Work Harder." POLITICO, January 29, 2015. https://www.politico.com/story/2015/01/scott-walker-higher-education-university-professors-114716.

McNutt, Marcia K., Monica Bradford, Jeffrey M. Drazen, Brooks Hanson, Bob Howard, Kathleen Hall Jamieson, Véronique Kiermer, et al. "Transparency in Authors' Contributions and Responsibilities to Promote Integrity in Scientific Publication." *Proceedings of the National Academy of Sciences of the United States of America* 115, no. 11 (February 27, 2018): 2557–2560. https://doi.org/10.1073/pnas.1715374115.

Millard, Drew. "There's No Such Thing as 'Productivity' during a Pandemic." *The Outline*, March 26, 2020. https://theoutline.com/post/8883/working-from-home-during-the-coronavirus-pandemic-is-not-a-recipe-for-productivity?zd=1&zi=ddfqlfn3.

Mountz, Alison, Anne Bonds, Becky Mansfield, Jenna Loyd, Jennifer Hyndman, Margaret Walton-Roberts, Ranu Basu, et al. "For Slow Scholarship: A Feminist Politics of Resistance through Collective Action in the Neoliberal University." *ACME: An International Journal for Critical Geographies*, August 18, 2015. https://www.acme-journal.org/index.php/acme/article/view/1058.

Musu, Costanza. "War Metaphors Used for COVID-19 Are Compelling but Also Dangerous." *The Conversation*, April 8, 2020. https://theconversation.com/war-metaphors-used-for-covid-19-are-compelling-but-also-dangerous-135406.

"Net for Slackers To Be Nation-Wide." *The New York Times*, September 2, 1918. https://timesmachine.nytimes.com/timesmachine/1918/09/02/98270704.html.

Newport, Cal. *Digital Minimalism: On Living Better with Less Technology.* New. York: Penguin Books Ltd., 2019.

Noguchi, Yuki. "8 Tips to Make Working From Home Work For You." NPR, March 15, 2020. https://www.npr.org/2020/03/15/815549926/8-tips-to-make-working-from-home-work-for-you.

Obama, Michelle. "Transcript: Michelle Obama's Convention Speech." NPR, September 5, 2012. https://www.npr.org/2012/09/04/160578836/transcript-michelle-obamas-convention-speech.

O'Connor, Brian. *Idleness: A Philosophical Essay*. Princeton, NJ: Princeton University Press, 2018.

Odell, Jenny. *How to Do Nothing: Resisting the Attention Economy*. Brooklyn, NY: Melville House, 2019.

Owens, Joseph. "Aristotle on Leisure." *Canadian Journal of Philosophy* 11, no. 4 (December 1981): 713–723.

Penn, Anita. "My Professors Are Lazy." *The Varsity*, March 17, 2015. https://thevarsity.ca/2015/03/16/my-professors-are-lazy/.

Pieper, Josef. *Leisure, the Basis of Culture*. Translated by Gerald Malsbary. South Bend, IN: St. Augustine's Press, 1998.

Porter, Tom. "Trump Shared a Tweet Mocking Biden for Wearing a Face Mask in Public – in Line with the CDC Advice That the President Routinely Ignores," May 26, 2020. https://www.businessinsider.com/trump-shares-tweet-mocking-biden-face-mask-coronavirus-2020-5.

Pychyl, Timothy, and Fuschia Sirois. "Procrastination, Emotion Regulation, and Well-Being." In *Procrastination, Health, and Well-Being*, edited by Timothy A. Pychyl and Fuschia M. Sirois, 163–188. Netherlands: Elsevier Science, 2016.

Ratcliffe, Susan, ed. "Linda Evangelista." In *Oxford Reference*. Oxford University Press, 2016. https://www.oxfordreference.com/view/10.1093/acref/9780191826719.001.0001/q-oro-ed4-00016802.

"Rich Kids Of the Internet." *RKOI Instagram Account*. Instagram. Accessed June 15, 2020. https://www.instagram.com/rkoi/?hl=en.

Ruiz, Michelle. "11 Tips for Work From Home Without Losing Your Mind." *Vogue*, April 6, 2020. https://www.vogue.com/article/work-from-home-tips.

Russell, Bertrand. *In Praise of Idleness: And Other Essays*. New York: Routledge, 2004.

Salles, Arghavan, and Jessica Gold. "The Problem with Comparing Health Care Workers to Soldiers on Memorial Day." *Vox*, May 25, 2020. https://www.vox.com/first-person/2020/5/25/21267541/coronavirus-covid-19-memorial-day-doctors-soldiers-nurses-health-care-workers.

Schwartz, Nelson D., Ben Casselman, and Ella Koeze. "How Bad Is Unemployment? 'Literally Off the Charts'." *The New York Times*, May 8,

Why It's OK to Be a Slacker

2020. https://www.nytimes.com/interactive/2020/05/08/business/economy/april-jobs-report.html.

Serhan, Yasmeen. "The Case Against Waging 'War' on the Coronavirus." *Atlantic*, March 31, 2020. https://www.theatlantic.com/international/archive/2020/03/war-metaphor-coronavirus/609049/.

Shippen, Nichole Marie. *Decolonizing Time: Work, Leisure and Freedom*. New York: Palgrave Macmillan, 2014.

"'Slacker Records' Drafted for War." *The New York Times*. Accessed June 6, 2020. https://timesmachine.nytimes.com/timesmachine/1918/09/29/109330352.html.

Smith, Kiona N. "Protesting During A Pandemic Isn't New: Meet the Anti-Mask League Of 1918." *Forbes Magazine*, April 29, 2020. https://www.forbes.com/sites/kionasmith/2020/04/29/protesting-during-a-pandemic-isnt-new-meet-the-anti-mask-league/#77aeca5412f9.

Speare-Cole, Rebecca. "Piers Morgan Launches Angry Rant at Britons Failing to Stay at Home." *Evening Standard*, March 23, 2020. https://www.standard.co.uk/news/uk/piers-morgan-good-morning-britain-rant-coronavirus-people-outside-a4394466.html.

Stack, Megan K. "Bravery and Nihilism on the Streets of Hong Kong." *New Yorker*, August 31, 2019. https://www.newyorker.com/news/dispatch/bravery-and-nihilism-amid-the-protests-in-hong-kong.

Stern, Alexandra Minna, and Howard Markel. "Pandemics: The Ethics of Mandatory and Voluntary Interventions." *The Hastings Center. Bioethics Briefings*. Accessed June 6, 2020. https://www.thehastingscenter.org/briefingbook/pandemic/.

Sutherland, Willard C. "Philosophy of Leisure." *Annals of the American Academy of Political and Social Science* 313 (September 1957): 1–3.

Tao, Chien (YuanMing) *The Selected Poems of T'ao Ch'ien* . Translated by David Hinton. Port Townsend, WA: Copper Canyon Press, 2016.

Tao, Yuanming. "Homecoming." Accessed June 10, 2020. https://fanti.dugushici.com/ancient_proses/70573.

Tomes, Nancy. "'Destroyer and Teacher': Managing the Masses during the 1918–1919 Influenza Pandemic." *Public Health Reports* 125, no. Supplement 3 (2010): 48–62. https://doi.org/10.1177/00333549101250s308.

Tsui, Bonnie. "You Are Doing Something Important When You Aren't Doing Anything." *The New York Times*, June 21, 2019. https://www.nytimes.com/2019/06/21/opinion/summer-lying-fallow.html.

Vannucci, Anna, Kaitlin M. Flannery, and Christine Mccauley Ohannessian. "Social Media Use and Anxiety in Emerging Adults." *Journal of Affective*

Disorders 207 (2017): 163–166. https://doi.org/10.1016/j.jad.2016.08.040.

Venkatraman, Vijaysree. "Conventions of Scientific Authorship." *Science* (2010). https://doi.org/10.1126/science.caredit.a1000039.

Wall, Brian. "'Jackie Treehorn Treats Objects Like Women!': Two Types of Fetishism in The Big Lebowski." *Camera Obscura: Feminism, Culture, and Media Studies* 23, no. 3 (2008): 111–135. https://doi.org/10.1215/02705346-2008-009.

Weber, Max. *The Protestant Ethic and the Spirit of Capitalism*. Translated by Talcott Parsons. London: Routledge, 2001.

Weeks, Kathi. *The Problem with Work: Feminism, Marxism, Antiwork Politics, and Postwork Imaginaries*. Durham, NC: Duke University Press, 2011.

Wilkinson, Alissa. "Pandemics Are Not Wars." *Vox*, April 15, 2020. https://www.vox.com/culture/2020/4/15/21193679/coronavirus-pandemic-war-metaphor-ecology-microbiome.

Wolf, Zachary B. "Forget Pork. Here's Why You Can't Buy Flour." CNN, May 2, 2020. https://www.cnn.com/2020/05/02/politics/what-matters-may-1/index.html.

Wollan, Malia. "At the San Antonio Food Bank, the Cars Keep Coming." *The New York Times*, May 26, 2020. https://www.nytimes.com/interactive/2020/05/26/magazine/coronavirus-san-antonio-unemployment-jobs.html.

Woods, Heather Cleland, and Holly Scott. "#Sleepyteens: Social Media Use in Adolescence Is Associated with Poor Sleep Quality, Anxiety, Depression and Low Self-Esteem." *Journal of Adolescence* 51 (2016): 41–49. https://doi.org/10.1016/j.adolescence.2016.05.008.

Zimmerman, Douglas. "San Francisco Forced People to Wear Masks during the 1918 Spanish Flu Pandemic. Did It Help?" *San Francisco Chronicle*, April 10, 2020. https://www.sfgate.com/coronavirus/article/1918-pandemic-masks-bay-area-california-15185425.php.

Zomorodi, Manoush. *Bored and Brilliant: How Spacing out Can Unlock Your Most Productive and Creative Self*. New York: Picador, 2018.

List of Films and Film Scripts

LIST OF FILMS

The Big Lebowski. Directed by Joel Coen. Universal Pictures, 1998. Film.

Clerks. Directed by Kevin Smith. Miramax Films, 1994. Film.

Dazed and Confused. Directed by Richard Linklater. Gramercy Pictures, 1993. Film.

Fast Times at Ridgemont High. Directed by Amy Heckerling. Universal Pictures, 1982. Film.

Knocked Up. Directed by Judd Apatow. Universal Pictures, 2007. Film.

Mac and Devin Go to Highschool. Directed by Dylan Brown. Anchor Bay Films, 2012. Film.

Office Space. Directed by Mike Judge. 20th Century Fox, 1999. Film.

Pineapple Express. Directed by David Gordon Green. Sony Pictures Releasing, 2008. Film.

Scott Pilgrim vs. the World. Directed by Edgar Wright. Universal Pictures, 2010. Film.

Slacker. Directed by Richard Linklater. Orion Classics, 1991. Film.

Zack and Miri Make a Porno. Directed by Kevin Smith. The Weinstein Company, 2008. Film.

LIST OF FILM SCRIPTS

"The Big Lebowski Script." *Scripts.com*. Accessed June 20, 2020. https://www.scripts.com/script-pdf/77.

"Clerks Script by Kevin Smith." *Daily Script*. Accessed June 20, 2020. http://www.dailyscript.com/scripts/clerks.html.

"Clerks Script." *Scripts.com*. Accessed June 20, 2020. https://www.scripts.com/script-pdf/5656.

"Dazed and Confused Script." *Scripts.com*. Accessed June 20, 2020. https://www.scripts.com/script-pdf/6451.

"Office Space Script." *Scripts.com*. Accessed June 20, 2020. https://www.scripts.com/script-pdf/726.

"Scott Pilgrim vs. the World Movie Script." *Scripts.com*. Accessed June 20, 2020. https://www.scripts.com/script/scott_pilgrim_vs._the_world_17641.

"Slacker Script." *Scripts.com*. Accessed June 20, 2020. https://www.scripts.com/script-pdf/18272.

"Zack and Miri Make a Porno Script." *Scripts.com*. Accessed June 20, 2020. https://www.scripts.com/script/zack_and_miri_make_a_porno_23941.

Index

Printed in the United States
by Baker & Taylor Publisher Services